EMANCIPATION
from SALVATION

R. DAX MAURICE

BALBOA.
PRESS
A DIVISION OF HAY HOUSE

Balboa Press books may be ordered through booksellers or by contacting:

Balboa Press
A Division of Hay House
1663 Liberty Drive
Bloomington, IN 47403
www.balboapress.com
1 (877) 407-4847

Because of the dynamic nature of the Internet, any web addresses or
links contained in this book may have changed since publication and
may no longer be valid. The views expressed in this work are solely those
of the author and do not necessarily reflect the views of the publisher,
and the publisher hereby disclaims any responsibility for them.

The author of this book does not dispense medical advice or prescribe the use
of any technique as a form of treatment for physical, emotional, or medical
problems without the advice of a physician, either directly or indirectly. The
intent of the author is only to offer information of a general nature to help
you in your quest for emotional and spiritual well-being. In the event you use
any of the information in this book for yourself, which is your constitutional
right, the author and the publisher assume no responsibility for your actions.

Any people depicted in stock imagery provided by Thinkstock are models,
and such images are being used for illustrative purposes only.
Certain stock imagery © Thinkstock.

Print information available on the last page.

ISBN: 978-1-5043-9284-6 (sc)
ISBN: 978-1-5043-9286-0 (hc)
ISBN: 978-1-5043-9285-3 (e)

Library of Congress Control Number: 2017918173

Balboa Press rev. date: 12/04/2017

TABLE OF CONTENTS

FOREWORD

This novel was intended to be an autobiography. After a professional editor reviewed the manuscript, I was informed that I could not use the real names of the organizations, schools, associations, restaurants, clubs, or people in the novel without written permission.

Therefore, to make a complicated task simple, I used fictitious names on everything. None of the places are for real, and none of the locations are accurate. All the names of people and organizations, schools, and associations involved have been changed to protect myself as well as them.

Since this labor changed manuscript from an autobiography to a novel, I also changed a number of the nonfiction circumstances to fictional events, so as not to leave a trail. I got carried away and even changed the name of the author to a pseudonym.

Even though this task was additional and necessary, I believe that it actually helped the evolution of the story. However, most importantly, the journals of my spiritual experiences are for real. The intimate chronicles of my metamorphosis which led to the emancipation from salvation to spiritual freedom are the real thing.

1

THE FOUNDATION

It was cold Wednesday morning, and Jack Frost had paid us a visit for the third straight night. My mother crept into the bedroom, but before she got to our beds, both my brother and I were awake, anticipating her 5:15 wake-up call. We both eagerly got dressed for the upcoming mile-and-a-quarter excursion. We dressed in the warmest clothes we could find, using scarfs and hats to cover everything but our eyes.

Mama gave us the final inspection before we headed out to the door. It was still dark outside, but we had our bikes ready to roll. My big brother was on his twenty-eight-inch bike, and I was on my twenty-six-inch. These were the older model bikes, the ones with the big tires and the backpedaled brake systems. We hit the deserted road and took off toward St. Christopher Catholic Church. We were altar boys, and this was our week to serve at 6:00 a.m. Mass. My brother and I were always dependable, and we took our duties as altar boys seriously.

We skipped breakfast because we needed to fast so that we could receive Holy Communion. Serving as an altar boy was one of the highlights of my childhood, since I was raised as a devout

Catholic. We were fortunate to have an excellent priest as our role model during that time. Also, my mother's first cousin was a priest, another first cousin was in a religious order, and her uncle was a member of a religious order. We came from a family with a history of ordained ministers.

When it was time for high school, I decided to go to the seminary in order to study for the priesthood. I chose an out-of-state seminary located on a multiacre spread in the hardwood forest outside Lexington, Kentucky. I spent two spectacular years at St. John's Seminary. It was run by the monks of the St. Julian order.

There I was fortunate to be influenced by the spiritual and pious countenances and auras of the priest, brothers, and monks of this religious order. The seminary was located adjacent to their monastery. We seminarians were normal high school adolescents. Most of us were there primarily for the adventure and secondarily for studying for the priesthood. I noticed that we behaved and obeyed the rules not out of fear but to honor the St. Julian priest, brothers, and monks, who honored us by allowing us to be semi-participants in their monastery. We had mutual respect.

In my summer job between sophomore and junior years, I interacted with regular, non-seminarian high school students. A couple of girls took a liking to me, and I developed a fancy for one of them. The novelty of this physical, mental, and emotional experience captured my imagination. I decided to leave the seminary. My life was about to change in many ways.

Because of my Catholic history, I was led to attend the regional Catholic high school, which was also a boarding school. You must remember that I was leaving the influence of the St. Julian monastery to be with yet another religious order. I was anticipating a spiritual atmosphere similar to that I had experienced at St. John's Seminary. But the actions and attitudes of the ordained clerics in my new school were everything but that. Thirty seconds after walking through the front door on my first day, I realized that this was not the atmosphere of mutual respect and honor of my previous experience. This place was run on the opposite virtues than those at St. John's Seminary.

The amount of unnecessary, pathetic cruelty performed under the banner of religious authority was overwhelming. My childhood belief in the infallibility of adults and the religious clergy of the Catholic church was quickly deflated and replaced with the knowledge that these clerics were ordinary men using fear to hide their insecurities and inadequacies. The saving graces of this ordeal were the patience and understanding of my parents and the wonderful friendships I made at that age.

One benefit from high school was that I received an excellent education. All of the teachers at St. John's Seminary were priests who all had the equivalent of PhD educations.

My new school had the reputation of being a premier college-preparatory high school, and in my opinion, it was. Because of the discipline, regime, and study habits that I acquired at St. John's Seminary, I was well prepared for their academic expectations.

After high school graduation and at the eleventh hour, I decided not attend the local university but rather leave home and go to a neighboring city and attend a smaller university of academic excellence. It was a choice that I have never regretted.

Because my high school running buddy and I decided to enroll at a very late date, we were put into a makeshift dormitory. The university housing rules back then forced all freshmen to live in an on-campus dormitory for the first year. To accommodate the latecomers and overflow, a two-story army barracks was converted into a dormitory. There were just enough students to fill the first floor. There were about thirty-two of us, and with the dorm being small and quaint, we got to know each other quite quickly. My buddy was my roommate.

Two weeks into the first semester, one of the guys on the floor decided that college was not for him, so he departed. In late November, we got news that he had been drafted and sent to Vietnam; he was killed shortly after his arrival.

Fortunately for me, I was well prepared for college. The majority of my courses during the first semester were the same as I had had in high school. The only difference was in college, a subject was covered in one semester, whereas we covered the same material in high school in one year.

This gave me the opportunity to become oriented into college life without the stress of academics. I also realized that if I did not study and pass, I, too, would be drafted like our dormmate three doors down. These two factors gave me the incentive and edge for my first year in college.

Following my first semester in the dormitory, the university housing committee decided to exempt all those who were living in the military barracks from living in the dormitories. We were allowed to seek residences elsewhere. This started the grand adventure of changing residence on a semester-by-semester basis. This enabled me to broaden my interactions with others as well as change my environment whenever I needed to.

After my first year in college, I was comfortable with my own approach to college life and academics. Because of my study habits, I did not have to worry about passing. Studying and learning were actually fun and enjoyable and part of the experience. And at that age, I had a bulletproof body, the coordination of an athlete, a fresh set of adrenals, and an imagination of infinite possibilities. If I had had the wisdom of the ages, I would have been scary.

Even though I needed to work in order to go to college, I found the time to join a fraternity. It was a wonderful experience. The intramural sports and other inter-fraternity competitions built fellowship. Another big plus factor that built fellowship was the ability to throw some outrageous college parties. Fortunately, this was before they passed the law that you had to be twenty-one in order to purchase alcoholic beverages. I guess the lawmakers realized if you were old enough to be drafted and killed in Vietnam, then you should be able to buy a beer. I developed many long-lasting friendships and wonderful memories through participating in a fraternity.

College was a time for me to develop new ideas nurtured by the responsibility of my own autonomy. I was committed to study during the weekdays. If I had an hour or two break between classes, you would always find me in the library. But when the weekend came, it was time to rumble.

During the course of my education, I change my major three times. My first major was general studies because I couldn't think of anything else to major in. I later changed to computer science because this university had one of the nation's best computer science curriculums. One night when I was studying, I realized that I could learn practically anything if I sat down and applied myself. It was that night that I got the urge to change my major to premed.

Premed was a grand adventure. I was fortunate to have excellent teachers at a top-rated university who presented to me a first-class curriculum in premed. I was given an excellent opportunity to learn. Every teacher I had was fair and willing to go the extra yard. I developed wonderful companionship with the guys in premed with me. We helped each other through. Most of my classmates became medical physicians, and I became a chiropractic physician.

I consider myself to have a slightly above-average, left-brained intelligence. I think my work ethic and my guardian angel pulled me through premed. I made As and Bs throughout my premed studies. I never was good at taking those big exams, like the ACT test, that evaluate your IQ. As a result, my med-cap examination score was mediocre. The dean of the medical school told me that my scores on that examination were the reason I was not going to be accepted into medical school.

Back then I thought it was a disaster, but it turned out to be part of Divine Spirit's plan for my destiny. My inner guidance made sure I went into the premed curriculum and I did not get accepted into medical school. I was fortunate not to be accepted into med school because I came to be a healer in the art and science of spinal energetics, osteopathic manipulation, acupuncture, nutrition, and other natural modalities.

I was born with a gift of healing and with an affinity for the energetic domain of healing through meridian therapy, also known as acupuncture. Chiropractic spinal manipulation is really an offshoot of acupuncture. It is called *Tui Nai*, or bone setting in acupuncture. Acupuncture is noted to be four thousand years old, whereas chiropractic is a little over one hundred years old.

After I left college and was not accepted to med school, I was like a ship without a sail or rudder. I did not know that chiropractic even existed. I moved back home and started looking for a job. I had two of the best employment agencies trying to help me find a job with my degree. There were minimal things that you can do with a premed degree beside go to medical school.

When I was running low on finances and hope, next door to the garage apartment I was renting, contractors were building an apartment complex. I went to investigate and found a construction job hanging sheet rock. (More divine guidance.) I very quickly learned the skill. Since I now had a skill that I could take anywhere, I called my cousin who was living in Honolulu, Hawaii, and asked him if he could help me get started there. He said he would help me out for a couple of months, but after that, I had to be on my own. I said no problem. I decided that if I was going to be miserable, I might as well be miserable in paradise, so I packed and left for Hawaii.

That was the end of phase 1 of my life. I had a wonderful childhood; I did not have a lot of money, but I was very rich in the quality of life, experiences, and character that money could not buy. My journey through high school was a mixture of simplicity for the first two years followed by a complexity of dynamics that helped me make important decisions that paved the way for the rest of my life.

College was a grand adventure of discovery. This adventure was a huge smorgasbord of different experiences, each one opening the door to a different and sometimes new aspect of myself.

The education was more than the academic preparation for my future as a healer; it was also the foundation for me to do my own creative thinking about many things in my life. I learned to believe in myself and began to pay more conscious attention to the whisper of Divine Spirit in my heart.

Throughout this phase of my life, even at a very young age, I was unquestionably being led through life by a guidance of a higher power, which was directing my destiny. I was mostly unaware of the significance of this guidance and how it strategically altered my decisions by its unique and mysterious ways to guarantee that I developed the necessary character and talents to fulfill my physical and spiritual mission.

The next phase of my life was about awakening to the advent of my spiritual consciousness, and to the awareness and development of my right-brain talents. These two elements led to the awareness of my healing abilities and to the introduction to some of my spiritual gifts.

2

PHASE TWO

My year-long sojourn to Hawaii was heaven sent. Peter, my cousin, was well submerged into the Hawaiian culture, and he enthusiastically orientated me into the expansive, free-spirited mind-set of the Hawaiian way. This attitude plus the magnificent beauty of the Hawaiian Islands was the perfect environment to heal my heart from the loss of a couple of important broken dreams.

During my visit, I blended work, play, and the spirit of adventure. I was able to backpack and camp on the islands of Kauai, Maui, and the Big Island of Hawaii, and I had numerous weekend adventures to the waterfalls and forest of Oahu. Every island had its own unique personality and venues, making each island tour a one-of-a-kind experience.

I also made it a point to consistently boogie board at Sandy Beach and Molokai Beach and a few beaches on the North Shore. I enjoyed spending Sunday evenings at Queens Surf, participating in the many different frolics of free expression and enjoying the magnificent sunsets brought to you by the expansiveness of the Pacific Ocean, which allowed no interruptions of this beauty.

It was there that I learned how to play a musical instrument and was introduced to many different spiritual paths of the Eastern philosophies. It was interesting to me that many of the spiritual concepts of the Eastern-based religions paralleled the mental concepts I was developing on my own by following the inner guidance of my heart. It was an awakening to the realization that I was never taught the history, sociology, geography, religious beliefs, or culture of half of the world.

These spiritual concepts validated many of my beliefs and answered every question I had about spirituality and even answered questions I had yet to ask. During my carefree investigation, I discovered one spiritual path that had absolutely no ceiling of attainment or restrictions on love. It was infinite and absolute in its expansiveness. I am still exploring this path.

There were a handful of people who made a lasting impression and will forever have a very special place in my heart. Their love, friendship, and memories will eternally be cherished. One evening, I realized that every dream I had ever imagined and everything I ever wanted to accomplish while in Hawaii was fulfilled. I got the inner nudge that it was time to return home. I had no idea on what was waiting for me back in Missouri.

Shortly upon my return, I met a drop-dead gorgeous lady who had a major impact in my life. Jennifer was the messenger who introduced me to chiropractic and to the spiritual healing philosophies. She was also a very talented Tarot card reader who introduced me to my right-brain talents and awareness.

Some people consider using the right brain and the accompanying awareness as being psychic. In my opinion, if you are a human being, then you have a right brain, and the use of the right brain is being psychic. I remember when I was first introduced to the use and interpretation of the right-brain impressions; this beautiful lady referred to it as being psychic, and I said, "Oh, is that what been psychic is? I have been psychic my whole life and never knew it." An internet investigation listed approximately 180 different psychic talents and phenomena, but to me, it's all variants of the same concept.

These psychic experiences and my interactions with this wonderful lady made me aware of many of my spiritual gifts and gave me permission to develop these gifts. It was also at this time that I became astutely aware of my healing hands and accompanying healing talents.

I entered chiropractic college two years after I graduated from the state university. I started chiropractic college with a renewed and healed spirit and with great expectations. I was academically ready after graduating in premed and was extremely confident with my newly found spiritual awareness, healing talents, and blossoming psychic gifts.

There were three major events that happened the first year I was in chiropractic college. During my freshman year, there was the switch from a strong chiropractic philosophy to a strong emphasis on academics. I saw the decline of the healing consciousness of chiropractic with the replacement of the strong academic medical model and approach. This was because of the political influence of chiropractic being accepted into Medicare. The insurance industry and politics forced chiropractic to become the medical model. This may be good or bad, but by the time I graduated from chiropractic college, chiropractic had loss its soul and healing consciousness.

Another important occurrence that totally directed my course of action for the rest of my freshman year was yet another event directed by Divine Spirit. I found myself in the library at every break. I was guided to the far left and back section, where there were not many visitors but where the old chiropractic books were shelved. The books were written by the pioneers who had a keen sense of healing awareness, blended with a unique intuitive knowingness and piercing insight into the energetics and neurology of chiropractic.

There were only about thirty or so of these books, and in my mesmerized state, I read every one of them. I arrived at the understanding of how spinal manipulation, neurology, and energetics work together to produce the miracles of old. To end this phenomenon, the day I was leaving the library after reading the last chronicle, I noticed a book on the shelf behind the librarian.

The book was about a methodology in chiropractic. This method seemed to be the closest healing technique that I summarized from reading all of these old chiropractic books of wisdom. I was informed that they were teaching this course off-campus, so I enrolled. About forty students from my class started the course, but only four finished. I was one of them.

As we were finishing the last syllabus of the course, I asked one of the practicing doctors if I could be his shadow in his office. He obliged. So twice a week for three years, I drove to his office to watch him use this marvelous methodology. As I became able, I would perform his examinations and take his x-rays as my contribution for his generosity.

My last story that happened during my freshman year sprang from my friendship with a senior intern. He was in the process of learning another advanced methodology. He would teach me how to do these procedures because he believed that if he knew the procedures well enough to teach me, then he knew it. He also taught me how to do spinal manipulation under the same theory.

By the end of my freshman year, I knew the two premier chiropractic techniques as well as spinal manipulation. Learning these clinical procedures came very easy for me. It was more like I was remembering instead of learning something new. From the clinical aspect, I was well ahead of my classmates.

During my second semester as a junior, we were allowed to see patients in the clinic as interns. As a junior intern, we were responsible for our own patients and did not attend to walk-in patients until we were a senior intern. By the end of the last semester of my junior year, I and one other classmate were totally complete with our clinical requirements. This had never happened before.

As a result, the school started a proctorship for us to work with a chiropractor in the metro area for our senior year instead of doing clinical rounds. This was to get us out of the clinic so the other interns could make their quota. I was assigned to a very talented chiropractor. Upon his recommendation, I would assist him on three days, and then I would go to help the other doctor for the other two days. I was becoming much grounded in clinical procedure.

After I graduated from chiropractic college, Divine Spirit had me working for a very charismatic chiropractor in a large city instead of opening my own practice in my home town. This was another divine occurrence and definitely a blessing because Dr. Wonderful taught me how to make money with my profession. Without his guidance, I would have made many mistakes in the business aspect of practice. After six months of study and working with this marvelous person, with his blessing, I bought a dwindling practice in another city.

I immediately implemented his business model along with my clinical expertise; within three months, I had my new practice at maximum capacity. This euphoria lasted for the next twelve years. I was on the top of the social consciousness success stories of my profession. I was driving a Cadillac, I had three boats (one for all occasions), I was taking many national and international trips for continual education seminars or chiropractic business, I was wearing all of the expensive clothes, I was a member of all the right clubs, I was doing the dance.

Part of my euphoria was the continual development of the spiritual awareness that I found in Hawaii and the spiritual gifts introduced to me by my beautiful lady friend. Even though I had many positive things happen for me during this time, my ego was on a pretty good ride. These experiences were building the circumstances and spiritual foundation for the hurricane winds of change that were coming.

From my experience, breakdowns or problems are necessary for growth. I needed a challenge, a breakdown, or a problem to nudge and sometimes force me to use my creative imagination to grow. I needed a major challenge to break me out of my comfort zone in order to change my approach from the mind-ego social consciousness to more of a heart-spiritual consciousness. I needed something to force me to pay more attention to the whisper of Spirit over the screaming cries of the mind-ego consciousness. There is more to life than social consciousness success.

I never saw the breakdown and future catastrophes coming because they manifested in a slow and balanced development. But looking back, I am more than glad that they came. They were actually an answer to my deepest and most sacred prayers. My prayers were about spiritual freedom and that infinite expansiveness and limitless love that I was searching for in all the wrong places.

3

Preferred Provider

The next phase starts in 1980s, with the propagation of the preferred provider concept. The insurance companies had a list of doctors who would agree to a financial cut in the delivery of their services for the guarantee of more patients.

It was a very ingenious concept, created specifically by the insurance companies in their continuous ploy to stop what they consider to be overutilization and to collect more and pay less, thereby generating profit at the expense of the health and safety of their policyholders.

Unfortunately, many institutions and physicians greedily abused the system. From my perspective, the insurance industry used this as an opportunity to set major restrictions for the purpose of stopping the abusers and for the opportunity to generate huge profits. It was a shame that all had to suffer because of a few.

As you may remember, you were given list of providers and told that these were now your primary health care physicians. This list was the name of the preferred physicians they would pay. If you agreed to accept the preferred provider as your physician, your payment was very little to no out-of-pocket expense.

But if you chose to go to a doctor you had been seeing for years, and this doctor was not on the preferred provider list, the insurance companies would either not cover their bills or you would have to pay a substantial out-of-pocket expense. There were a few people who were lucky enough that their physicians were on the list and were able to maintain their health care relationship with them.

Also, remember, there were numerous restrictions and a huge list of limitations that would limit your physician's ability to give you the best of his knowledge and skills. There were many times when the decision for your health was not in your primary physician's hands but rested with the insurance companies' representative.

These representatives chose what was appropriate, chose what they would pay for it, and chose what diagnostic and therapeutic procedures were acceptable. Because of the exorbitant financial cost to the policyholder if they disagreed, many patients went with the decision of the insurance company instead of their physician.

Some very important health care decisions were being made by someone in the insurance company with the primary intent of saving the company money. Someone would not authorize covering certain "unnecessary" tests and procedures needed to make the proper diagnosis. Another practice the insurance company used was forcing the use of less expensive, lower quality surgical implants and other similar cost-saving procedures. All of these decisions were at the expense of your health and the quality of health care delivered.

This nightmare continued until the lawmakers realized that many of the necessary and important tests that were needed to make a proper diagnosis were being refused or rejected as unacceptable or unnecessary by the insurance companies, and some of these decisions resulted in misdiagnosis. Lawmakers also noticed that insurance representatives would refuse to pay for procedures that were necessary after the diagnosis was made. These actions are, in my opinion, a form of malpractice. After the abuse hit home and was affecting the politicians' families, friends, and constituents, the lawmakers were motivated to take action.

From the doctor's point of view, most of the chiropractors within my region, who I knew were good physicians, were working at optimal capacity. The idea for us to sign up on the insurance companies' list and receive less payment for the work which we were now doing seemed quite absurd. Therefore, most of the good practitioners did not sign up and thus found their pants down when the time came to implement the preferred provider concept.

The chiropractors in my region who signed up were the ones who lacked either the social or clinical skills to maintain a thriving practice. Preferred provider was the life raft to save their sinking ship. When the time came for the switch from the standard and usual co-pay insurance protocol to the preferred provider ordeal, these chiropractors who signed up received their dream of a thriving practice.

A number of my patients came back, despite the extra expense, because of the inadequacy of their treatments. A number also wished they could come back but could not because I was not on their preferred provider list.

During this unique period in time, I was trying to reinvent myself. I discovered an academic academy for chiropractors in the

Tulsa area. An ingenious chiropractor formed this school under these circumstances to help take chiropractors to a new level of healthcare delivery. His ideal was formed from the knowledge that the average medical physician's bill was 80 percent diagnostic and 20 percent cure, compared to the average chiropractor's bill, which was 20 percent diagnostic and 80 percent cure. His theory was if you increase your diagnostic skills, you could supplement your lost income because of the preferred provider ordeal.

I joined the Academy, and one weekend a month for a little over three years, I attended school. I learned the art and science and mastered every noninvasive diagnostic procedure available to the healthcare system and to chiropractic. The knowledge and skills that I obtained were invaluable. It opened up huge areas of clinical awareness and clinical procedures that were not available in the chiropractic schools.

We were also introduced to the medical model of physical rehabilitation, which was surprisingly different from the chiropractic approach. Again, I learned the art and science and mastered the diagnostic and therapeutic protocols to make this transition. Practice was fun, but I did not notice any remarkable improvement in clinical outcome from this model. Nothing could come close to the clinical excellence of the energetic and the primary respiratory motion approach to spinal and musculoskeletal rehabilitation.

The last step that the Academy offered its students was the knowledge and the necessary personnel to set up a legal diagnostic and therapeutic clinic under the watchful eye of a medical physician. One attorney studied the legalities and became an expert on how to set up and run a facility legally so that you could collect for your services rendered.

This change was necessary because if a chiropractor was to do the exact same diagnostic or clinical procedure as a medical physician or physical therapist, they would not be reimbursed for the services, even though they were within his scope of practice. However, if you would bill the procedure under a medical physician's name, you would be reimbursed.

I stayed with the Academy until I finished their program. On Saturday evenings after hours, there were sharing sessions to strategize on the next steps to stay ahead of the preferred provider attempts to restrict the healthcare delivery system.

The new concept that came up for chiropractors to adapt and survive the preferred provider concept was to become a physical therapist. This was the most secure way to get paid by the insurance companies. Chiropractors were continually being restricted and limited to the quality and quantity of the services the insurance company would allow and reimburse, whereas physical therapists were not restricted for the same services that were administered for the same diagnosis.

In Atlanta, there was a chiropractor who had a remarkable talent of continually thinking outside the box. I would not see him if I had a physical backache but would definitely talk to him if my practice had a backache. He caught wind of the concept that physical therapy trumped chiropractic in the reimbursement arena, so he set up a physical therapy school to co-exist with the existing medical school at the University of Allied Health Sciences of the Dominican Republic.

I joined the third class for a degree in physical therapy at that university. There are tens of thousands of chiropractors in the United States, but only about fifteen took advantage of this opportunity.

4

Dominican Republic

ttending physical therapy school in the Dominican Republic was no picnic. We had to cram in one semester of school in two weeks. We sat in class for the exact time to equal the precise number of classroom hours that any physical therapy student in the United States would require. We had school from nine to five, six days a week. The rest of the evening was study, study, and study. Sunday was free; I might indulge in a couple hours of beach fun, but I had a more important task at hand: to study and pass the upcoming test. These two weeks were a grueling experience.

The school provided teachers who were actively teaching in the United States to teach us the physical therapy courses. We had medical physicians or PhD-level teachers teaching us the science courses. We had an orthopedic surgeon from the United States who taught us the orthopedic course. We had tests that were as hard as any that I have taken in my undergraduate and doctoral-level studies.

One of the faculty held a position as the director of physical therapy at a hospital in the United States. He was so kind as to allow a number of us to obtain our hospital internship hours at the hospital. I became aware of the remarkable services rendered by physical therapists in the hospital setting, especially the acute-care and postsurgical division.

I was lucky to find two very well-organized and clinically superior physical therapy clinics to work at during my internship. These two facilities could hold their own in comparison to any clinics in the United States. I am well convinced from working both sides of the street that physical therapy performs some services that chiropractic does not, and chiropractic performs some services that physical therapy does not. If these two disciplines ever come together, they would find that both disciplines could add effectiveness to each other's modalities. The winner in this junction would be the patient. Unfortunately, politics has these two healing arts scared of each other.

When it became time to apply for an application to obtain a physical therapy license in the United States, one of the requirements was validation that the school the applicant attended was up to American standards. The certification board for the physical therapist organizations in the United States reviewed the University of Allied Health Science and declared that this school was inferior.

Everyone who attended this university already had a doctoral degree, plus the university had qualified teachers in every aspect of the curriculum and met every requirement of every physical therapy school in United States. All students graduating from this university were declared unqualified to sit for licensure exams in the states that use this certification board as their selection committee. Thankfully, there were a handful of states that did their own certification process, which gladly accepted the students who had graduated from the University of Allied Health Sciences, Dominican Republic.

Politics, in my view, makes rules governed by greed, power, and fear. As an example, this certification board closed the door in many states for anyone to obtain a license within that state if they graduated from the University of Allied Health Sciences.

It was said that the national certification board stated, "If we do not stop this school, we will have the chiropractors taking over physical therapy." The regulatory boards are designed to protect the public and insure the quality of health care. In this case, the ruling was to protect their pocketbook and their employer's pocketbook.

This was strike one against the domain where social consciousness, motivated by greed, fear, or ignorance, triumphed over what is right, truthful, just, and honest. According to the rules and regulations, the University of Allied Health Sciences was an above-board, genuine academic institution meeting all of the necessary requirements for acceptance. Recognition of this program was rejected because the students in this program were doctors of chiropractic.

I did not obtain my physical therapy license, as most of my colleagues did. During that time between my graduation and taking the physical therapy national board examination, I got married and was in the process moving to Oklahoma.

When I arrived in Oklahoma, I became aware that chiropractors there can practice acupuncture, if certified. Since I was very familiar with the acupuncture system, I began pursuing my acupuncture certification through the Oklahoma State Regulatory Board for Chiropractic.

Although I intended to take the next board examination for physical therapy, I became so fascinated with acupuncture and my new marriage that I did not bother. I pursued these two new adventures instead of physical therapy.

However, I have absolutely no regrets that I obtained inside information on physical therapy. My opinions of the physical therapy profession are based on experience instead of hearsay.

Many chiropractors are taught to fear physical therapists because they will take over chiropractic if not held in check (sound familiar?). I have a lot of respect but absolutely no fear of the physical therapy profession, as many chiropractors do.

In my interactions with the physical therapy profession, I became aware of the intra-vaginal procedure that is taught by the National Physical Therapy Union. Because I was pursuing and developing my talents with acupuncture, I put that information on the back burner. But years later, when I was having a clinical discussion with a therapist, he mentioned his results with this procedure.

What grabbed my attention from this conversation was that he related this procedure to the science of the primary respiratory motion of the spine. The primary respiratory motion is the study of the biomechanics of the central nervous system through the action of the meningeal system.

The anatomy and physiology of the meningeal system has an important influence on the central nervous system, on overall health, and on the ability to recuperate from injury and disease. It is especially important in spinal biomechanics.

The primary respiratory motion, in my clinical experience, is the foundation of the chiropractic profession. You can shorten the treatment time considerably, obtain symptomatic relief quicker, and reach stability longer by addressing the primary respiratory motion firsthand.

In many incidents, when you have a spinal condition that did not respond favorably to surgery, medication, physical therapy, or chiropractic, it is because the meningeal system and its relationship with the primary respiratory motion has not been addressed.

The science of the primary respiratory motion, its importance, and its influence on many aspects of our health is taught primarily by an outstanding institution for the physical therapists and massage therapists and by another organization for the chiropractic profession.

Shortly after graduation from chiropractic college, I studied the meningeal system concommitted with the primary respiratory motion and the unique clinical approaches to diagnose and address this pathology. I attended two weeklong symposium sponsored by this organization.

The information obtained was invaluable and has consistently stood the test of time and trial. Unfortunately, it is a lost science in chiropractic practice. This clinical approach is not taught in many chiropractic colleges, and the intra-vaginal procedure is only embraced by the medical profession.

The National Physical Therapy Union teaches correcting pelvic floor muscle dysfunction in chronic pelvic pain by the intra-vaginal procedure. By addressing the science of the primary respiratory motion within this procedure, the effectiveness of this clinical approach and the decrease of treatment time, especially in the difficult cases, are noted.

5

OKLAHOMA

I practiced in Oklahoma for over ten years. During that time, I lost my chiropractic license because I performed the intra-vaginal procedure I learned in physical therapy school on a consenting adult and obtained the expected and predicted clinical results. There were only five patients that I performed the intra-vaginal procedure on. Their clinical picture follows.

The first patient was a woman I had been treating weekly for three years. She came to me because she had a chronic case of rheumatoid arthritis. Her medical physician had her on seven drugs for this condition. The iatrogenic effect of this medication left this patient in a state of chronic fatigue.

After working with this patient, she was able to take herself off all but two medications, and those she self-regulated until she could get the symptomatic relief she needed without the debilitating side effects. Her physician was so pleased that he wrote a prescription for her to receive chiropractic treatments on a weekly basis.

The weekly treatments were able to keep her rheumatoid condition abated while she was able to function in life at her normal capacity. However, she reported that she still had this persistent low-grade chronic headache. She had this headache for twelve years. I tried the intra-vaginal procedure on her, and her headache disappeared within three hours and never returned. Results like that got my attention. She kept coming in until I left Oklahoma.

The second patient I performed this procedure on was a health care provider who had a slip-and-fall accident and landed on her tailbone, which jammed her sacroiliac and lower back articulations. After weeks of treatment, I was able to reduce the quantity of pain and sometimes get her out of pain, but was never able to obtain stability. The results only lasted twelve hours or so. The company physicians said that she would be a candidate for spinal surgery if her condition did not approve in two weeks.

She asked me if I was aware of this procedure. I told her yes. She requested that I try it on her. I did. She got immediate and permanent relief. She was immensely grateful because not only did this procedure alleviate her condition and obtain stability, it also saved her from spinal surgery, which both she and I knew would be the beginning of a lifetime of misery. She returned bi-monthly for maintenance treatments

The next person I performed this procedure on had been my patient for over three years. One day, she mentioned to me that since her hysterectomy two years ago, she had been suffering from bladder incontinence and pain on intercourse with her husband. I mentioned this procedure, and she elected to have it performed. Following this procedure, she reported that her bladder function was now normal and pain while making love with her husband was gone. She continued to come in.

The fourth patient I performed this procedure on came to me after seeing her medical physicians and physical therapist. Treatments by these two allopathic disciplines produced no clinical or symptomatic results, and her condition was getting worse. This patient could not walk, run, or climb up or down stairs or get in or out of her car without excruciating pain in her groin and hip region. Clinical trials with me only produced temporary relief, but she was happy because at least it was finally not getting worse.

I mentioned this procedure, and she elected to have it performed. Immediately following this procedure, she obtained immediate and substantial relief. Upon her next treatment, she said most of the pain was gone; however, there was residual pain. She requested that I do this procedure again. I did, and she received permanent relief and stability. She came back for a few follow-up treatments, after which all was well.

The fifth and final patient I performed this procedure on came to me as the result of an accident. She had seen a medical physician, another chiropractor, and a physical therapy and received no relief. Her medical doctor referred her to an orthopedic surgeon, who performs a spinal fusion on her midcervical vertebrae. The fusion did not take.

The surgeon would take an x-ray every six weeks to evaluate the status of the procedure. After the second set of x-rays the physician said that the fusion had not worked. There would be another x-ray evaluation in six weeks, and if the fusion was not healing, she was going to have a second surgery.

The probability of the second attempt at cervical fusion being successful is very low, for the same scientific reason the first attempt was unsuccessful.

A surgical fusion is a trauma, a very controlled and skillfully performed trauma, but nevertheless a trauma. The patient is re-traumatized in an area that has already been severely traumatized twice. The possibility of greater neurological and orthopedic complications resulting from the second attempt at cervical fusion is very high. This is when she came to see me.

This patient reported that she could not hold anything in her right hand. Not only was her extremity weak, but any use of her arm caused referred pain into her neck. Examination findings showed that there was gross muscle weakness in the right arm as a result from the surgery and accident. The manual muscle testing examination did produce pain in her neck whenever the test was performed. She had severe muscle spasms throughout the spine, with a marked decrease in range of motion throughout her spine. She was in trouble.

Upon her seventh treatment, I mentioned this procedure, and she elected to have it performed. The procedure released the gross meningeal tension, causing immediate relaxing of the vertebrae in her middle of her back to the point that a spinal manipulation was possible and successful. As a result, the surgical fusion in her neck was able to heal, thereby eliminating the need for the second surgery. The muscle weakness in her right arm had complete recovery, as documented in her future medical records.

It would raise the question as to why someone who received the clinical results that saved her from the expense, trauma, and gamble of another spinal fusion surgery would reward me by reporting me to the chiropractic board of examiners and initiate a complaint to have my license revoked.

This patient did not return for further treatment. Obviously, her motivation pivoted from maximum medical recovery from her clinical problem to maximum pursuit of a million-dollar malpractice insurance payoff. This individual did accomplish monetary gain from this maneuver.

In her attorney's unethical, immoral, deceitful, and slimy (the words of other attorneys) plot to recover the money (and split the recovery fee), he used the chiropractic board as a pawn to achieve that goal.

6

ADMINISTRATIVE LAW

This following was brought to me by someone who is very familiar with the procedures of the professional boards and administrative law courts. His report validated my experience.

These boards of examiners are at times above the law. The accused are not innocent until proven guilty. They are assumed guilty and must prove their innocence. The board does not have to prove anything with facts or back up any of their accusations with any scientific proof. Their opinions do not have to be validated, and they usually supersede facts. They are able to make statements and judgments for which they are not academically qualified, and they are considered above reproach.

Typically, what dominate a board's decisions are the political biases, hearsay, and dictates from the bully of the board. They have their own personal agendas. Everything is filtered and judged through the politics of that agenda and the power structure of the board.

There are laws that are protected by our Constitution when it comes to civil and criminal courts. In administrative law, boards of examiners are exempted from our Constitutional protection. These boards are allowed to make their own rules and to govern themselves by their interpretation of these rules. They have the authority to declare what is moral or ethical. They at times grant themselves the authority to declare and legislate what is lawful when there is no law.

Something like the intra-vaginal procedure could be very legitimate, within the scope of practice and within the rules of standard of care, validated by scientific literature and peer-reviewed literature, and obtain specific and predicted clinical results as dictated by science, and still be declared by the board to be inappropriate.

If an individual challenges the board's decisions, they have the opportunity to have their case heard in administrative law court. The administrative law courts run on the same principle. In these courts, the accused rights are not protected by our Constitution. They have the authority to make their own decisions not based on law, and not based on facts, merely on opinion.

Many times, in situations with the board and with administrative law, many of the decision depend upon the politics between the judge, the district attorney, and the defense attorney.

If you would investigate some of the procedures, you would see how some people do very questionable things, hire expensive but excellent trial attorneys, and get away with it. Unfortunately, someone who commits a slight misdemeanor may get the maximum penalty if they are not represented by an excellent attorney.

Even though good decisions do come from the different boards and administrative law courts, because of their design, they have the potential of acting as a genuine kangaroo court.

Those accused by the board of a violation have to represent themselves. They have to hire an attorney and use their own money, whereas the board has an attorney appointed to represent them, which is paid for by the state.

If the accused challenges the board's decision, the case can be heard in an administrative law court. Again, the accused has to foot the bill for his attorney from out of his pocket, whereas the board uses attorneys who are paid for by the state.

That is what happened to me. I hired an attorney who would fit what was available within the limits of my credit card. He was a very ethical person and very knowledgeable about chiropractic, but he was like me, very naïve, and thought that truth, honestly, integrity, and justice would triumph over lies, deceit, and politics.

After witnessing the proceedings, attitudes, and atmosphere of the first hour of my two-day hearing, I knew that I had absolutely no chance of winning this trial. For example, the first order of business was to establish the foundation of the trial. Every objection and ruling went to the district attorney's advantage. My attorney wanted to submit a sworn deposition from a physician who was very knowledgeable about the intra-vaginal procedure. The doctor declared that there are volumes of research papers published regarding the science and effectiveness of this procedure. He referenced three during his deposition that validated the necessity of this procedure for this patient's clinical picture. Submission of deposition denied.

On the other hand, the testimony of the doctor who was the state's witness was riddled with hearsay and contradictions. Even though he had five years to research his "four crates of scientific literature," he presented no scientific evidence to back his opinions. An example, he stated that I should have taken my own x-rays. A ten day old radiology report of the cervical spine by a certified medical radiologist was unacceptable. This is contrary to standard clinical protocol. (He also said that there is no such thing as lymphatic drainage massage, a common massage technique.)

As another example, I did not answer the district attorney's question with just a yes or no response but explained the logic of my answer; he claimed that I was non-responsive, and the judge agreed. The judge had his mind made up, regardless of what evidence was presented. The trial was a formality.

The board rescinded my license for sexual misconduct because I performed an intra-vaginal procedure that they declared was unproven. It was irrelevant that the National Physical Therapy Union taught this same procedure fourteen times that year, and I was introduced to this procedure during my studies at the University of Allied Health Science.

I supplied the board with a legal document that grounded this procedure in scientific and peer-reviewed literature. The document validated my decision with solid scientific-based clinical symptoms that validated the necessity of this procedure. However, the board also had their minds made up; they too were not interested in the facts.

I did perform this procedure on a consenting adult in a professional manner and got the expected and positive predicted clinical outcome.

They claimed that I was sloppy in the delivery of this procedure. I did not obey the unwritten rules in administering this procedure. In this judgment, they were correct.

The board declared that this procedure was sexual misconduct, even though the administrative law judge testified in front of the board that in his opinion, I "did not do this procedure for sexual gratification because it is based on science." This statement was shocking to hear because the judge recommended that I lose my license.

During the administrative law trial, I explained the relationship of the meningeal system and primary respiratory motion to the spinal biomechanics of this particular case. The judge understood the academics as they related to the procedure and realized the clinical significance of how and why I obtained the clinical results that I did for this patient.

The board ruled that chiropractors do not do this procedure in Oklahoma; in Louisiana and other states, it's okay, but in Oklahoma, chiropractic doctors who are trained spinal specialists cannot do this procedure. Only physical therapist and medical physicians are allowed.

For me, this was strike two for trust in social consciousness.

7

I NEED TO CHANGE

People do not easily change their old habits, beliefs, thoughts, and emotional patterns that they developed during their childhood, primarily because of fear and lack of awareness. They fail to realize that most of these postulates they live by were given to them by the church, state, and other authorities, for the primary purpose of controlling them.

Note that many religious authorities proclaim that these rules are divinely dictated from God. However, we know that historically, many of the postulates are based on religious beliefs that are blended with social, geographical, political, and economic conditions. These are a few of the conditions that make the rules different among various religions.

In many instances, state authorities enact laws to govern the masses and to protect the weak from the strong. This is not so bad because it does lay down regulations and ideals of social ethics and social morals that create some order out of chaos. However, many of the social mores and ethics are not illegal, accorded to state-created law.

It is interesting to note that authorities normally exempt themselves from the rules they make to govern others.

Most people feel powerless over these given conditions. They are held in check by some form of fear. This fear can be generated by social, economic, legal, or religious influences.

Many people do not challenge obsolete habits, thoughts, and emotional patterns because they do not know that they have a choice. They do not realize that most of these postulates are not their own. They take for granted that these postulates are the way it is. They are so wrapped up in making a living and enjoying a little leisure time that they do not investigate the origin of these postulates. Or they would rather not be bothered.

Other times, people do not change because these postulates have produced personal ego satisfaction. They have found some sort of social, economic, or political reward, which is appealing to them. They have found approval, security, and control within these conditions.

Some people change old habits, beliefs, and thought patterns because they have to. They realize that if they do not change, they will continue to manifest into their lives the same misery that they are now experiencing. The old habits no longer work for them.

This process is relatively difficult. How do you facilitate necessary changes? There are many ways to change; one of the best ways is to have the earnest desire to change, take action, and find a support group to assist you.

The magnificent group called Alcoholic Anonymous is an organization where people who are committed to changing their lives for the better are given support to do so. There is space created for people to investigate the postulates given to them and the opportunity to change.

I chose to re-examine these patterns of my beliefs because I also wanted something different to manifest into my life; I discovered I had lived by the moral, religious, legal, and ethical ideals given to me during my childhood. They had proven to be inadequate as I matured and did my own thinking. They did not stand my test of spiritual consciousness. I felt compelled to re-examine these rules.

For me, it appeared that the negative influences dominated the positive. It appeared that the lust for power, the greed for money, manipulating the truth with deceit and lies, and the display of vanity were the motivating factors of most people's actions. These powers seemed to corrupt people's dedication to contentment, honesty, truthfulness, and integrity.

I have noticed that guilt, blame and shame are the emotions people use to assert their beliefs onto others in order to control individual freedom. However, they are adamant about others not doing the same thing to them. They are the ones that want to run your life when they can't even run their own.

I knew that I could not eliminate these negative forces that motivated people's actions that manifested their materialistic code of ethics for success in the social consciousness arena.

It became imperative for me to invent new ideals for me to live by that would triumph over these negative influences. In order to create different postulates of a higher virtue, I had to take a different perspective. I had to create a different starting point. I was being compelled to follow my inner guidance.

In looking back into the past, I can recognize some important turning points in my life. Somehow, I can't quite remember the logic of why I made these decisions, but I do know that somehow, there was an invisible spiritual force that motivated me to make specific decisions that led me to my destiny.

I had a vision of where I wanted to end up, but the way I perceived of arriving at my final destination was totally different from Divine Spirit's plan. I must say I was definitely better off with Spirit's plan than mine. Spirit's plan was not as easy to follow, but it was always the best. I really do not know how I actually got there, but here I am, and I do know that I am exactly where I need to be in order to shape and mold myself into the person I am.

From a social point of view, these situations could be termed as setbacks or unfortunate events, but from the spiritual point of view, they were perfect. There are no mistakes, only lessons.

There were specific incidents that opened the door to my latent talents and gifts that I was to develop and use to serve my fellow beings. Some incidents were to develop my physical talents, emotional attitudes, new thought patterns, and new ways to look at reality. Others were to motivate me and to catapult me into the awareness of my spiritual destiny.

In many ways, this incident with the Oklahoma chiropractic board was a major turning point in my life. This incident crumbled every stability factor that I believed in. Because of this board's ruling, I eventually lost my livelihood, my marriage, my house, my pets, my hobbies, and some acquaintances, but most importantly, I lost my faith in truth, integrity, ethics, justice, and the legal system.

I had hung my hat on the premise that if I did my best to help my patients with an open heart and with pure intent and within the law, then all would be well. I never imagined that greed, lies, and deceit, and the total lack of ethics and integrity, would trump my ideals. I knew that this happened in politics and to other people, but not to me. I felt betrayed and let down.

Everything seemed to be taken from me. I know that I have an immense talent and gift of healing. I could see, sense, and feel energetic and neurological energy with my spiritual insight; I could easily conceive and understand complicated energetic as well as other neurological concepts. I intuitively knew how to blend them together to know what to do to get a person well faster and better, and with longer lasting results. I could clinically succeed where everyone else would fail.

Many times, I had insight into the answer on how to help a person that no one else could find. I was diligently looking for the correct questions to the answers I had already found. Even though I prided myself on my talents and my gifts, I supplemented them with many hours of study, of trial-and-error observations above and beyond the usual in order to develop my healing gift to a high level.

One of the main problem with being a genius is that you are judged by colleagues whose knowledge is usually elementary, obsolete, and antiquated. They do not think out of the box and are unaware of new clinical approaches. Even if this new information is based on pure scientific research and is published in peer-reviewed literature, they are usually down upon the things they are not up on. Many times, they do not know that they do not know.

So I was forced into early retirement. At first, I thought it was the end of my world, and it was, in a way, for it ended my attachment to social consciousness and too many of the ideals given to me during childhood.

Actually, it turned out to be a huge blessing. It turned out to be a turning point in my life that had a major influence on my spiritual destiny. My new perspective on life was beginning to be forged.

I had nothing to lose; I had already lost it all. My new adventure into the rest of my life would be more than I could ever have bargained for. A new life of observation in wonderment was about to begin. I was drawn into a future framed by Spirit.

8

THE CHANGES

So what was left for me? After losing everything that I thought was valuable, I moved back to my hometown. Fortunately, I was able to stay with one of my siblings for a while, and I lived on the inheritance money that my aunt left me. Besides getting over the emotional trauma, I spent a lot of this time developing new perspectives and ideals to live by.

During that time, I purchased a FEMA trailer at an auction. I bought it with the idea of converting it into a fishing or hunting camp. Little did I know that I was going to live in that trailer for a little over a year. So I went from a $250,000 house in suburbs of a metropolitan city in Oklahoma to a $2,500 FEMA trailer in rural Little Paris, Missouri.

I went from a six-figure income to Social Security. I went from shopping at Dillard's to shopping at Goodwill. I stayed very low-key and kept to myself, focusing my time on my work, my family, and a few friends. This was an opportune time to reinvent myself and to start focusing on new ideals and new priorities.

I wanted to change how it felt to be me. I wanted to change my thoughts and emotional patterns. I wanted to desensitize the memories of my past. The old me had served me well up to this point, but now it was time to move on. It was time to change.

What was important now was different. The old image of being the chiropractor extraordinaire had lost its appeal. The chase to satisfy my projected image and ego of being the successful chiropractor, making a lot of money in order to purchase things that are not really necessary but convenient and to propagate my social image, was no longer important.

I found that I did not need to know all the big shots; I did not need to drive the fancy car or wear the expensive clothes. Been there, done that; I enjoyed that, but it was time to move on. This annihilation of a major part of my ego was a huge blessing.

Control-alt-delete; now it was time to reboot. What was the new program that I wanted to install? How did I go about finding this new direction, these new postulates, this new foundation on which to build my new vision of reality?

I had to make alterations on how to achieve my spiritual goals of reinventing my life. I was forced to take a different approach to life. I was being pushed to walk through different doors that I had chosen to ignore because of the ease of operating within certain domains that were familiar and quite ego satisfying.

The old ways of operating and looking at things needed to change. Not that the old ways were wrong; they were just obsolete and ineffective.

It was still important to me to keep up my spiritual responsibilities to develop my healing talents to the best of my abilities. This meant the continual development of my academic knowledge with my spiritual gifts so I could make a difference in people's lives. This is still part of my primary mission.

The major shift was in developing the capacity of my spiritual heart to recognize love and beauty. With the obliteration of a major part of my ego, there remained a void I chose to fill with the change of perspective on how I subjectively looked at life. Even though I was already on a spiritual path, there was a huge shift of energy that propelled me to witness and recognize this deeper love and beauty by using my right brain primarily instead of my left brain.

Another important gift of walking through the door of change was allowing myself to heighten my awareness of the importance of the now, to appreciate the present moment, to be present to a domain of life that I had been overlooking.

These shifts opened a huge arena of appreciation for me. The development and the blending of my spiritual heart and right brain with the accelerated opening of my spiritual eye presented to me a kaleidoscope of beauty that in many incidents were far beyond the description of words and could only be experienced and known through the spiritual heart.

I became astutely aware that in order to appreciate the beauty in all things, I must accept the beauty within myself. I chose to allow this beauty to be recognized and accepted in the forefront of my new perspective of observation.

I began to focus on the now and on the images that I was receiving from my spiritual eye and interpreting with my right brain. I began to be aware of the oneness of it all: to meld with the connection of the beauty that connects all things. My inner communication with all things on the invisible side was blossoming.

I found within myself an increased level of stillness and peace that seemed to keep the spiritual heart and spiritual eye open. This peace permitted me to see the joy of life in everything, in plants, trees, grass, bugs, and animals, and within people in many new ways. I witnessed in both their physical and spiritual realities the expression of the Divine Spirit flowing through them.

I felt a deep knowledge that my life was in the hands and guidance of Divine Spirit. I became aware that I am important in God's eyes simply because I am. It deepened my appreciation that I am protected by this divine voice of God.

I developed new ways of observing the mundane. I was steadily becoming the perpetual energy of the smile.

I observed that I would lose this joyful song of the heart if my consciousness became stuck in the memories of the past or in the anxieties for the future.

I found it imperative to develop the art of forgiveness. Forgiveness became for me the path to loving myself enough to forgive all who had trespassed against me. Forgiveness would give me spiritual freedom and expand my heart back into the smile energy and back into the now.

To the offenders, I learned to give detachment and goodwill, or maybe better said "good luck." However, I also remained conscious that I was not exempt from maintaining good boundaries.

I developed the premise that forgiveness is a selfish gift that I give myself. I allowed more of the beauty that I had been witnessing and experiencing within my golden heart by releasing the energy of the past and setting myself free by living in the present moment. Doing this would help me manifest more joy, more knowing, more stillness to cherish the presence of the divine flow within and to observe the light and essence of God's voice.

One day, I had an experience that allowed me to realize the importance of the now; in that moment, I totally released and forgave anybody and everybody for anything or everything that I had declared unjust or unfair to me. This forgiveness including myself; in that total immersion into the now, I experienced the immensity of spiritual freedom.

The power of that experience implanted within me a knowingness of God's love. I will forever do my best to not allow anybody or anything to interfere with the deepening of that kiss from Divine Spirit. Nothing is worth the loss of that presence. The purity of that love that I experienced was timeless and eternal. The choice to forgive became a no choice; it was a given.

It became imperative to me to take the high road of love and to trust in the knowing that everything is taken care of by Divine Spirit for my spiritual emancipation. Just be still and listen to the whisper of the divine in my spiritual heart.

In the mental realm, I realized that no one is exempt from the karma of his beliefs, thoughts, and actions, including myself. On judgment day, the lords of karma do not care who your daddy was, what politicians you knew, what positions you held, how much money you had, how big your badge was, how big your gun was, how you rationalized or justified your behavior, or what you did or didn't do. The lords of karma are not fools. It is a 100 percent just and impeccably honest court.

This court does not use the rules and regulations of religion or the laws given by the state to pass its judgments. The many criteria used in the evaluation of a soul's actions in this court are in so many ways superior to the social consciousness.

So what became paramount and forefront of my new goals was my budding awareness and the deepening of the perspective about my spiritual reality as soul and that connection to God and Divine Spirit. I learned about the spiritual beauty that has always been there, behind the noise of the sensations of the body, the chatter of the mind, and the stimulation of emotions. This immense beauty was hiding behind the many veils of the vanities of the ego.

The beauty that I found was discovered within the stillness of the now, perceived through the third eye, and translated by the right brain. This beauty came with the recognition of the presence of the flow of the divine through my spiritual heart. It beseeched me to make this flow of Divine Spirit through my heart, my beloved.

9

LIFE IN LITTLE PARIS

I found myself retired and living in a FEMA trailer in Little Paris, Missouri. This rural community was about twenty-five minutes south of a major city. The most remarkable thing about my new environment was that it was in the country. It was quiet and peaceful, and the few human neighbors that I had were wonderful.

Transitioning from a beautiful $250,000 home in suburban Oklahoma to a $2,500 trailer really wasn't that bad. I was now free of my mortgage, utilities, taxes, and insurances, plus all the business expenses. I automatically had a $6,000 a month raise. My little trailer was very comfortable and with the other amenities, I had everything I needed, especially an extremely low monthly overhead and solitude.

I signed up to receive Social Security. With my checks from the monthly distribution from my investments, I had enough money to cover all of my living expenses plus a little left over. I did not have the cash flow that I used to enjoy, but I was wonderfully happy and joyful.

The solitude and the stress-free living was the perfect environment for me to develop and focus on the creation of my new perspective on life. Everything was slower, and living in the country with cattle as most of my neighbors, I became tuned into a different rhythm much closer to nature. I was able to perceive and observe many new and subtle energy domains, which paralleled the development of my new spiritual insights.

During this time of reinventing my ideals and perceptions, I was very selective in what I read in regards to my relationship with Divine Spirit. I was careful to whom I talked about spirituality and what audiotapes I listened to and which discourses I studied. I preferred to read a few well-chosen books three or four times than to read many books.

During this time of peace and solitude, I contemplated spiritual concepts. I was diligent in performing the spiritual exercises that were presented. I dedicated quite a bit of my time and energy into the discovery of the spiritual realities within and beyond the physical, mental, and emotional realms.

I became conscientious in developing new mental habits to replace the old ones. Since the mind functions very effectively with habits, I made it a point to reprogram my new mental perspectives and postulates so they would become automatic.

I also made it a point to be astutely aware of my emotional state of being. Emotions are very powerful and usually are the motivation of my thoughts. When I would catch myself running on an old emotional attitude that did not complement my new and expansive spiritual awareness, I would stop and then choose the happiest and the most heart-expansive emotional attitude to match the situation. I was inventing a new model to be me.

During this time, I was also led to investigate different energy systems not presented in the traditional acupuncture curriculum. I spent hours researching and studying many unique and somewhat abandoned aspects of energetic healing as they relate to meridian therapy. I spent countless hours collecting data and then analyzing and synthesizing this information to build an academic model to fit within the known facts of meridian therapy. I wanted to make this modality a logical, reasonable, and reproducible method.

The energetic concept of meridian therapy has to do with the distribution of the universal life force, or chi. The same spiritual energy that runs the universe also runs the body. The ideal is to have a balanced distribution of Chi to all areas of the body. I spent months of trial and observation of the many different approaches and catalyzed them with creative insights.

This exciting investigation initiated the writing of books that would document the efficiency and effectiveness of this healing methodology. From that little trailer in the country, I wrote and self-published four books all related to applied energetics.

10

THE CHRISTIAN INFLUENCE

D uring the time I was living in Little Paris, I met a very remarkable person.

My new friend was a very devout Christian. Because of her remarkable intelligence and her persistence in study in the Bible, she was knowledgeable about the Christian Scriptures. She would often use the Bible to validate her point of view and to create for herself a highly ethical, compassionate, and meaningful life. She was a person of her word, honest, trustworthy, and very committed to walking the talk of her religious beliefs.

It was quite beautiful and heartwarming to listen to her discourses. She was pouring her heart and soul out to me, trying to explain her Christian point of view. I could only agree with her logic because from my point of view, she was remarkably accurate.

From my perspective, a major part of her belief system lived in the science of the mind. The mind works by a set of laws that is logical, reasonable, and predictable, and it works for everybody. You do not have to be a Christian for it to work. It works for everyone, even the agnostics and the evil. However, the Christians do have an edge; let me explain.

To simplify the complicated, we will say for the purpose of this discussion that the mind is composed of two sections: the censor division and the executive division.

When our minds receive raw physical, mental, and emotional data, this information goes through the censor division of the mind, which acts like a filter. This filter interprets, evaluates, and passes judgment on the information received. This raw information becomes altered to fit within our belief system; this modified information then goes to the execution division to manifest the commands of the censor division.

The censor division of the mind has the responsibility of interpreting and judging our experience. This section is composed of our belief systems; our emotional responses; the fears of approval, security, and control; and a few more interesting emotions of fear, along with the memories of our past experiences, plus the influences of pain and pleasure.

The censor division is the master of the left brain. The left brain primarily interprets reality related to space, time, and the energy of matter. It can only pull from past experiences and stored information to create and maintain our identity, and to secure our future. That is its purpose.

The left brain only knows itself through the ego. Thus, the ego defines our sense of self. The ego is created by identifying with things outside of itself and from memories of past experiences.

Through the ego, we identify with our jobs, the type of car we drive, the house we live in, our dress, our religion, our success, and our failures. The left brain's job is to create and maintain the identity of the ego.

To see an example of how the censor or filter system works, let's look at a manifestation we agree to call a red coupe automobile with a V-6 engine and white leather interior. One person may love the red coupe, and another may think it is a piece of junk. Both have their own reasons for why they like or dislike this particular vehicle. Both people think their opinion of this vehicle is reality, but it is not.

Their opinions are only their assessment coming from their left brain's filter. Each assessment is formed from their unique and individual experience and what they were taught to believe about this product. Their opinions are an illusion because the red coupe just is.

Their opinion about the car is about their individual viewpoints, and their opinions are about their perceptions and not necessarily about the car. We assume that everything is the way we see it. Everything is not the way we see it. A dozen people will have a dozen different opinions about the red vehicle. The vehicle is just a red vehicle.

If you begin to observe that we already have automatic opinions on just about everything, it becomes apparent that our assessments are grounded in past programming. Fortunately, this process proves our minds are working. We should not discord our evaluations, analysis, or judgments of our automatic assessments but start to become aware that we have them.

The integration of the right brain into the censor division adds a new dimension. It is like adding an additional filter between the left-brain censor and the execution division.

The right brain is the opposite of the left brain and knows itself through the stillness of the mind and the cessation of time; the right brain operates in the now. through the right brain, the soul, the spark of God which we truly are, can express Divine Spirit and experience the qualities of love, joy, and peace. The left-brain censor does not recognize these experiences without the soul adding this through the right brain.

To summarize, the censor division is composed of the analytical mind/left brain and the soul/right brain. The censor has the job of passing new experiences through our belief system. This includes the sensory perceptions, emotions, and commitments created by our beliefs. This can also include the soul viewpoint, which will include love, joy, and peace into the equation. This filter is an ever-changing composite of our ego and past experiences in both the left-brain and right-brain realities.

The interpretations and perceptions exiting the filter system create our vision of reality, and the executive division expresses this vision. The executive division is very powerful in executing the commands from the censor division, thereby manifesting our beliefs.

The executive division is why we always get what we pray for (or something close to it). If we are persistent with our vision or prayers and take enthusiastic action, the executive division will automatically deliver our desires.

The commitment to our beliefs, which drives what we manifest in our lives and how we interpret what we receive, is again run through our filter system that supports the beliefs. It's a perpetual cycle.

This is the law of manifestation. Speaking, both internal and external, creates our reality and our manifestations. What we speak is driven by our thoughts and emotions and beliefs. Everything in our life is a by-product of our belief systems and our speech.

Our beliefs drive our commitment. The magnitude of our commitment to our beliefs, opinions, and desires determines the focus of our power. Commitment is the strength of our desire to manifest something in our lives. Commitment determines where our attention goes and where our energy flows, which in turn determines what grows into manifestation.

My Christian friends have helped me upgrade my filter system. We have many similar beliefs, but through my observing of them using the laws of universal mind consciousness, or the law of manifestation, they helped me upgrade the quality of my filter. Because the laws are the same for all religions, their commitment helped me rekindle some of my commitments that I was taking for granted or was paying little attention to.

People always create from within their own set of beliefs. Everyone has their own set of rules, experiences, and beliefs to create their subjective story and to validate their subjective reality.

These beliefs are created from the set of possibilities given to us by church, state, and other authorities that are derivatives from the laws of universal mind consciousness. However, some people create new possibilities from the universal laws that are outside the box of the given set of possibilities called social consciousness.

The edge that I saw that some Christians have resides in their belief system, which is part of their censor filter. They have so much faith, confidence, and belief that Jesus will help them, and of course, by law, a form of it will manifest.

Their left-brain censor is void of the possibility that Jesus will not manifest for them their prayers. They do not realize that they actually produce the matrix for this experience to manifest for them.

They consistently praise Jesus or the Lord for their interpretation of a God-sent manifestation, which from my understanding has nothing to do with Jesus but is business as usual under the law of manifestation of the universal mind consciousness. To me, they are giving praise and glory to the universal mind consciousness that works through our censor filter systems and the executive system of our brain, regardless of the religion.

Their immutable faith and belief in Jesus is part of their censor. It is a wonderful thing, and in my opinion, more good things come from this than bad.

My beliefs come from a different set of beliefs created from the realization that I am soul, and soul uses the law of universal mind consciousness as a tool, but I do not consider this consciousness as the source.

Both perspectives are right for the individual, and neither perspective is wrong. Everyone is on their unique path back into the sacred heart of God. Who am I to second-guess Divine Spirit's plans for another or for myself? The only thing I can offer another is my opinions from my experiences and my goodwill.

I very shortly realized that I was investigating a whole new domain of spirituality that the Christian faith really understood little to nothing about. I was trying to talk to my friend about apples, but she only knew about oranges. She was adamant about the nonexistence of apples.

The more I listened to her and her friends share their stories of their beautiful faith, the more I appreciated their contribution to my spiritual development.

During this time in my quest to reinvent myself, many new spiritual experiences led to the accelerated development of my spiritual eye, right-brain awareness, and perpetual attention to the now. I was trying to make sense of this new area of spiritual experience.

When I was trying to make sense of my expansive relationship with God and Divine Spirit, my beautiful Christian friends helped show me what God is not. Their constant examples helped me realize the many dimensions of what God is to the Christian faith, but what I was observing and experiencing wasn't what they were saying.

There is nothing wrong with that. But for me, there was something beyond the manifesting power of the mind that I needed to know about. There was something beyond Christianity that I was being led to investigate. I was about to be shown; the curtain was getting ready to rise.

11

THE CHIROPRACTIC ARREST

During this period, as an energetic healer, I was utilizing the acupressure method I developed to treat a small number of clients in Little Paris. I was constantly observing the effectiveness of this method to ensure that what I was delivering could walk the talk or could be improved in some way. I also observed that because of my new spiritual disciplines and perspectives, the depths, effectiveness, and power of the healing sessions had increased.

My appreciation and observation of the body's energetic currents and my ability to see, feel, sense, and know had increased exponentially.

Healing is my gift and my God-given talent. My love language is touch. I use healing as an outflow of love. It is overwhelmingly beautiful to be able to touch people in a very specific and precise method to bring about the increase in the flow of Devine Spirit through their energy field, thereby reestablishing wellness. This gift has been a consistent blessing for me to share.

The Missouri State Police did an undercover investigation of my healing business.

The detective investigating the complaint sent in two fake patients to gather evidence to build a case. The fake clients wrote reports of their healing experience that were obviously subjectively biased, and they left out a very important fact in their report: They forgot to mention that they signed an informed consent document.

The informed consent document was overlooked by the investigating detective, along with another very important document. It is called the law, the Missouri Practice Act.

I made a point to have everyone sign an informed consent form before I started a healing session. This was to alert the client of my education and to let them know that I was not license to practice chiropractic in the state of Missouri.

This form further stated that "the client understood that these healing sessions are intended to enhance relaxation, reduce discomfort caused by muscle tension and improve the flow of Divine Spirit through the energetic systems. The purpose was also to educate me to possible energetic blockages that could interrupt this harmonious flow of spirit that may create pain and dis-ease."

Continuing with the language of the informed consent form:

"These sessions are safe and non-invasive. There will be gentle manual or mechanical stimulation of acupressure points that may restore the harmonious flow of spirit through the energetic systems of the body. The intent is to make you feel better.

"I understand that these healing sessions are not a substitute for any type of medical treatment, chiropractic, acupuncture or medication. I am aware that there will be no diagnosis rendered and no medication prescribed. There will be no acupuncture needles inserted.

"If I feel uncomfortable for any reason during the healing sessions I will let the healer know immediately."

This informed consent form was carefully constructed. Everything that the Missouri Chiropractic Act says that chiropractic is, the informed consent says that I am not.

Nevertheless, one day in late October, when I was coming back to the office for my next client, I opened the door to find six armed state troopers there to arrest me for practicing chiropractic without a license. I told them that I was a healer and not a chiropractor. They answered that because I had instruments that some chiropractors use and I intermittently do "spinal manipulation," then I am practicing chiropractic.

I learned that in order to ascertain the truth, I take a story and either prove it or disprove it with facts. The investigating state trooper logic was backwards. He took the fact that because I had some instruments that are utilized by some chiropractors, therefore, I was practicing chiropractic.

The facts are some of the instruments that I had in my office are used by every healing professional, not just chiropractic. Are the physical therapists, the massage therapists, the osteopaths, the naturopaths, the acupuncturists, and the medical physicians who use these instruments guilty of practicing chiropractic without a license?

The other issue, a grade five joint mobilization, is called thrust joint manipulation by the medical profession. It is called osteopathic manipulation by the osteopathic profession, it is called naturopathic manipulation by the naturopathic profession, and it is called Tui Na or bone setting by the acupuncturist and spinal manipulation by the chiropractors.

Spinal manipulation is only a trademark name of chiropractic. The clinical practice of the procedure of the great five joint mobilizations is utilized in many healing arts under a different name. If an osteopath performs this procedure, is he practicing chiropractic?

The investigating police did not care about these facts. They were bullies with badges; they had the guns and the authority to create any fictitious story and declare it true. I immediately realized that their minds were closed, and they were unable to hear the truth. Therefore, the best thing to do was to surrender to the experience.

Luckily, I saw my colleague in the hall and asked her to call my brother in order to handle the situation. Then the police handcuffed me, put me in the back of a car, and took me to jail.

Jail is designed to be a very negative and distasteful experience, which it is. For example, the temperature in the jail is so cold that most of the jailers wear jackets. Prisoner are dressed in very lightweight coveralls, not designed for warmth. Inmates are seated in a chair and are not allowed to talk. Jailors are in total control, and most have a chip on their shoulders. You are totally at their mercy. They are not in a rush to do anything. The intent is to keep you in jail for at least six hours. It was physically exhausting to spend six hours in a deep freeze.

I was emotionally devastated. I had made it a point to be as legal, legitimate, and aboveboard as I possibly could. I was not hurting anyone. In fact, I was using my God-given healing gift to provide service and relief to many people who could not find help elsewhere. I was working hard to make a positive contribution to my clients' lives.

I was mentally and emotionally destroyed. I felt betrayed. Evil, fear, and greed had triumphed over good intentions and good action again. Nothing made sense. Why was I here? I did not break any laws, nor did I hurt anybody. What had I done to deserve this? I was not a criminal. I felt like I was the victim of a witch hunt. If helping people is wrong, then nothing is right. What is going on with all the shady businesspeople, dirty politicians, and drug dealers who own the police force? Why are they free and I am in here? Questions like this were coming up as I tried to make some kind of sense from this ordeal.

I tried to still myself in order to get into the now, to quiet the mental and emotional monkeys going rampant within, but it was to no avail. I was blindsided by injustice and could not find my balance. The normal ecstasy that I find in my spiritual exercises during the benediction with the light and spiritual sound of God was escaping me. I could not calm myself enough. However, there was a knowing that the hand of God was once again disrupting my serenity to prepare me for the winds of change that were to take me on another quantum leap into the spiritual realities that I was eagerly exploring.

There was too much chaos to figure out anything on the physical, mental, emotional, or spiritual domains. I just had to endure this nightmare of insanity until it ended.

I was finally release at 11:30 that night. I was physically, mentally, emotionally, and spiritually numb. It was a tremendous relief to see my brother and my girlfriend; they immediately showered me with love and compassion. However, I was in a land of nothing.

The nothingness that I normally experience is the region that has everything in it. This nothingness is accompanied with bliss and with light and essence straight from the heart of God. This nothingness was the antithesis of the other. This nothingness had nothing but death within. It was surreal; my surroundings were like a morgue. My mind refused to think and make sense of my existence. I remembered only saying one thing: "There is nothing for me here."

My brother and girlfriend reached out to rescue me from this stasis. Both offered me their homes and companionship for the night. However, I wanted to be alone with myself in the environment of solitude, where I felt safe and comfortable. I vaguely remember, as if in a dream, driving home to my little trailer in the country. I do not remember falling asleep; I don't even remember praying that night. I do remember one thing: repeating the phrase, "There is nothing for me here."

That phrase became the new topic and theme of my next step in my spiritual quest. Spirit had very abruptly prepared me with the correct attitude and commitment to take a bold step into the unknown world of beauty that lies within my sacred heart. The charges were dropped, and the case was dismissed. However, without that experience, it may have been years before I would have the determination to investigate and discover the many spiritual worlds that exist.

If there is nothing for me here, then where do I go? How do I get there? I had to continue reinventing my spiritual realities.

12

DAYS AFTER THE ARREST

I recuperated physically, mentally, and emotionally from this experience much quicker than my brother, my girlfriend, and my family.

The next morning when I woke up, I called a few friends in Oklahoma, with the intent of trying to discover the spiritual purpose of this experience. For something of this magnitude to happen in the physical reality, it only means that one door is closing for another one to open in the spiritual domain.

It wasn't that important what my friends actually said; it was the love coming from their hearts complementing their trust in the Divine Spirit's plan for me. Those conversations were able to put me back into the saddle quickly and with the assurance that all is being taking care of by the divine power of Spirit.

One of the primary spiritual lessons from this ordeal was to let me know that I was ready for the next step in surrender. It reminded me of the story about the trapeze artist. To go from one trapeze to the other, you need to let go of one in order to fly unattached and in midair to the other to progress forward. I was being prepared to give up the more deeply embedded concepts and conditions taught and accepted as the whole truth to me in my childhood and to replace them with a broader and freer vision.

The next day, in my contemplative prayer, I heard the soft whisper of the intuitive hint to reread a few of my old favorite spiritual books. I went into storage and found my box of stored reading. I found two of my old friends and became reacquainted with them. I reread them three times with a new level of wonderment and intensity.

The primary points that stood out for me from these readings were the presence of our beloved spiritual traveler and the existence of the joys and glories of heaven, which are hidden within the stillness of our heart and soul. Until we start looking for and developing our inner spiritual self, the hidden treasures will only stay good ideas. The reality of the spiritual heavens will stay as something to talk about but not to live within.

Another important concept that presented to my newly awakened consciousness was that there are very specific and precise ways to find the treasures of heaven that live within. The states of consciousness of these heavens and their spiritual realities are very real and exist within very specific and scientific/spiritual laws. Many of these laws are similar to the physical laws we live within on this planet Earth. But many are different.

All the readings noted specific and precise disciplines that need to be followed in order to develop the awareness and to live within these heavens while at the same time living on earth. The statement of being in this world but not of it becomes a reality bigger than life. It's not just a saying; it becomes a knowing.

I can actually experience and become quite familiar with the heaven I will reside in once I leave my physical body. But I definitely had to want this experience and be ready with a whole new level of wonderment to follow Divine Spirit with total faith, confidence, and belief into the next step. I was now more determined to continue to reinvent a new way of life and a new way of looking at reality.

Regardless of what religion you are now following, it is my opinion that if you follow the light and spiritual sound of your religion, and if you are ready to replace many of the mental concepts and replace new insights and beliefs of spirituality, you can find this immense freedom, wisdom, and joy. It lives within you now.

I cannot share with you all of my discoveries, but I would share with you some insights and some of the disciplines that I learned that awakened within me the immense beauty of these inner heavenly worlds.

Remember that after that horrible physical experience, I walked away with the commitment that there is nothing for me here. I was through with living in this world, where I believed in the illusion of social conscious righteousness. What I was now looking for was the righteousness that came from a higher level of being and integrity.

How do I find it? How do I make it real? How do I make the knowing part of me become like breathing and my heartbeat?

For me, the first step into this new reality was already in my face. There is nothing for me here. I was so ready to let go of whatever was necessary from the past. I was ready to discard everything that I considered useless, antiquated, and obsolete and part of the illusion instead of the new spiritual reality.

I was ready to do whatever it takes, release whatever is necessary, add a whole new dimension of observation in order to meet the real person responsible for my happiness (or my unhappiness). I was ready to meet the mystical side of myself and discover what is real and what is the illusion.

13

I AM SOUL

The first important door that my spiritual guidance invited me through was the door of indifference. By being indifferent, I became still. Being still, I released and became detached from many of my old ideals. I was then able to reinvent a higher viewpoint based on love, forgiveness, and the flow of Divine Spirit through my spiritual heart.

The by-product of indifference is freedom. This freedom allowed me to put my attention elsewhere and make the spiritual changes I always wanted to but never knew how to achieve.

What I thought was important then compared to what I declared is important now, was on a quick-paced job of exchange that I hope will never end. The road of this journey goes forever upward. This journey helped me make the shift from the outer materialistic environment, which is dominated by the ego and materiality, to the inner subjective self. There within, I could find the love, beauty, ethics, and freedom that I seek and want to live by.

This viewpoint is living in the knowingness that I am soul having a physical, mental, and emotional experience. This knowing would replace the viewpoint that I am Dax, and I have a soul. Now it is, I am a soul having a Dax experience.

I needed to desensitize myself from the trained postulates of my early socialization and upbringing and switch to the spiritual viewpoint of soul. This requires constant vigilance of the now and the awareness of the automatic judgments from the workings of the mind.

From the stillness that complements the now, I have a choice to reinvent my subjective story of what is happening to a more uplifting, expansive, and freedom-giving outlook. This new attitude automatically allows contentment to enhance enjoyment of beingness and the knowing trust in the working of Divine Spirit in my life.

This freedom of reinventing my subjective story of reality brought an inner song to my heart. As I followed this melody, it led me deeper into the light.

For me, indifference was the path to the stability and the growth of this inner light and spiritual sound within my heart. It appeared to me that the more light and spiritual sound that I allowed into my heart, the more of the old programming I was able to release, and the easier it was to see the beauty in all.

I became aware of deep levels of mental entrapment that kept my ego first priority and thus prevented me from seeing these unique rays of love. I was ready to expose these demons. They were expelled by the light and spiritual sound of Divine Spirit at my command.

I was able to see beauty in more areas with less effort and in many domains where I never saw it before. This magnificence was always there, but I was unable to experience it until I became indifferent to the old viewpoints of life and replaced them with soul's viewpoint. Indifference created the space for this new spiritual viewpoint to show up and become a new part of my being. This change allowed me to observe the same objective happening, but now I was free to create a new inner subjective conversation with myself.

I became responsible for my well-being. I can now override the old judgments, prejudices, and ego-based thinking and replace it with indifference in order to allow a deeper peace, stillness, and appreciation into my life.

With this new level of freedom and this new viewpoint, I can create a new me. Even though chaos is still all around me, I can now choose a new way to experience and deal with it.

14

THE MANY FACETS OF INDIFFERENCE THE CYCLES

The subject of indifference is huge. It encompasses so many aspects. I do not know where to start. I found it was a very important discipline in my spiritual emancipation. Keep in mind that my primary goal of studying indifference was to free myself of the old social consciousness and to establish in its place the new spiritual consciousness.

One of the primary things that I noticed in my journey of exchanging social consciousness for spiritual self-realization was that there was a cycle. There was a period of experience, followed by upheaval in which new choices, new mental and emotional changes, were created that primarily led to greater surrender to the knowing that Divine Spirit is in charge. There would be a short period of rest as these changes became part of me, and then the anticipated and prayed-for upheaval would cycle again.

I would notice through my discipline that it would be easier to stay vigilant and indifferent during certain situations. But as soon as I got comfortable, there would be another spiritual lesson for me to learn. There would always be new dimensions of indifference for me to become stable within, but at a higher level of love and beauty.

One interesting phenomena in this journey is that I would intermittently experience a huge kiss of love from Divine Spirit. This ecstasy would cause major upheavals, which would initiate me releasing a large and stubborn portion of my security blanket of ego.

The process of releasing one security to replace it with another form of security (but of a higher spiritual value) was bittersweet.

When I was letting go of one trapeze to fly to the other in order to move forward, for a while, I was stuck in space with nothing but my faith, confidence, and belief in Divine Spirit that the other trapeze will be there and I will catch it.

After a few cyclical episodes, I started to anticipate with delight this region of not knowing as indifference spearheaded the physical, mental, emotional, and spiritual changes that enhanced the awareness of self as soul. When I was in this region of unknowing, I believed that I would know what I needed to know when I needed to know it. My responsibility was to make the necessary choices and changes that would get me to the next rest point. I was not interested in hitting a home run. Spirit's design of consistent, steady change was okay with me.

From my spiritual readings, my study of the audiotapes, and my contemplative prayers, I continually had an inner vision of what my spiritual goals were. I willingly gave myself permission to be a student, which meant I gave myself permission to make mistakes during the learning process. Throughout this journey,

I was constantly upgrading my vision of spiritual enlightenment, but I had no clue how to get there. I just knew that I had to keep allowing and trusting that Divine Spirit will guide me there in a balanced way.

I made it a point to release the old materialistic me for the new, more expansive, spiritual me. Everything I wanted to leave and everything I wanted to become depended upon me changing and controlling my emotions and thought patterns. This meant that I had to continue creating new beliefs and postulates to live by.

I used a few selected audiotapes to orientate me into the change. I listened to them on a daily basis. They were my travel companions; I listened to them when I played my computer games to relax in the evenings. They helped me focus onto the new outlook that was being established and growing within.

I made it a point to do selective spiritual reading and contemplative prayer on a daily basis. I had to; I was ready for emancipation, and what I was starting to experience in my endeavors was wonderful.

It took constant vigilance to my thoughts and to the song within my heart to change my viewpoint from social to soul consciousness. Because the mind is a machine of habit, I was diligent in forming new habits; I noticed that it took less focus to achieve this vigilance. The new perspective was starting to become automatic.

I noticed that by constantly training myself to focus on the good, and by becoming increasingly indifferent to others' opinions and judgments, more good and peace came into my life. In addition, having boundaries became increasingly important; I needed to be constantly aware of discernment to know when to have boundaries and when it was better to be neutral.

If I wanted more freedom, I had to give it to myself and to others. I needed to forgive others so others could forgive me. Again, this meant more freedom. I also realized that the only person I can control is me. I can control my subjective reality by changing my attitude, my viewpoint, and the story of how I interpret the facts or experiences that show up in my life. I discovered that I am ultimately responsible for me.

I would occasionally use what I called "focus remembering" to remind me about why and what I was leaving. This reminder encouraged me to keep going into this new world of subjective reality. Intermittently, I would remind myself, there is nothing for me here.

It is quite a wonderful deep breath of fresh air to give up the should and should nots and to accept life as it comes. To accept the ups and downs with an attitude of indifference and the choice to subjectively create a new story gives blessings of joy, fulfillment, and love instead of the old.

It is uplifting to exchange beliefs; I realized that beliefs are a combination of thoughts and emotions. Most of the beliefs I was taught related to the physical world and to social consciousness. What I was now pursuing was a spiritual consciousness that leads to unique and beautiful worlds laying hidden behind the left-brain limitations.

When I had routine experiences of dimensions and realities beyond space, matter, and time, I realized that the beliefs formulated by indifference, the awakened awareness of the vibrations of the spiritual eye, and the song of the spiritual heart interpreted by the right brain of knowing were more holistic. They surpass the knowledge and memories of the left brain in beauty, wisdom, and freedom because they are not limited by thoughts. They live in the knowing and not in knowledge.

The incentive to go into the new spiritual vibration of light and spiritual sound/essence was becoming stronger incentive than what I wanted to leave.

Throughout this metamorphosis, there was no one I could talk to about my new level of awareness and the many new realities that I would get glimpses of. Sometimes, these glimpses were so powerful that I could only experience three to ten seconds of that specific vibration or energy of sublime love. Other times, they would last for fifteen to twenty minutes; occasionally, they lasted for hours upon end. The duration and nature of the experience depended upon what Divine Spirit knew that I needed. My job was to supply the time, energy, and effort and to allow the guidance of Divine Spirit to rule.

Even though I could not share the intimacy and details of these experiences with my close friends and family, they noticed the results and commented on them. Most of the time, I seemed happier, fun-loving, optimistic, and at peace. Remember when I would take the next step? I would be in a new domain and for a while chaos ruled, until I found a new balance. It was always worth it because the bar was always rising. The viewpoint was expanding where freedom abounded.

Freedom is seeing the whole picture. It was becoming easier to be indifferent to the conditioned automatic response. It was becoming easier to choose my new story. I am responsible for creating the script of my life. I am responsible for the new subjective viewpoint that creates the space to experience life in the now.

This freedom allowed me to see the beauty within people; it was easier to find contentment and peace with life. Freedom is the blending of the outer objective "is-ness" with the inner subjective state of "being here now."

15

THE MANY FACES OF INDIFFERENCE CHANGE ATTITUDES

I t was time to continue to create new conversations, a new story about what I was objectively observing. It was time for me to continue to establish new postulates, which would give me more spiritual freedom, more love or goodwill for others, more forgiveness, which would open my heart to give and receive more of the blessings of Divine Spirit.

It was the continual experience of progressive learning on how to blend the right-brain awareness with the left-brain memory and knowledge. This blend allowed a new plateau of being that was uplifting and expansive. I was inventing a new perspective to observe and experience the ups and downs of life. I was consistently inventing a new me that I liked. Indifference for me was my starting place, the first step to change.

Most of my new choices came from my relationship with that mystical light and sound that was being developed within me by my focused attention on the now and stillness. This relationship made it possible to develop a deeper relationship with the presence of Divine Spirit within my spiritual heart.

I had to be careful that I was not creating for myself a new distinction in social consciousness instead of a new platform for spiritual freedom. There were a number of distinctions that I would use as my spiritual GPS.

One was my intent. I noticed my spiritual heart gave me joy, not the action. When I gave love to myself and to others, I was happy and joyful. I noticed there was joy in being aware that I am worthy of love because I am. There need not be a reason. I noticed that I can be loved and not be happy, but when I give love, I am.

It is sometimes difficult being the conduit for the flow of Divine Spirit through my heart without compromise. That's why it is called unconditional love. The primary reason I allowed love to enter my heart in difficult situations is because to stay connected to this current of divine love is my joy.

If my new decisions gave me a sense of expansion, awareness, peace, joy, stillness, and beauty, and if my body and emotions agreed with these assessments, then this decision would be good for me. On the other hand, if I got the inner feeling that these actions would cause a contraction of the spirit; anxiety; worry; a negative emotion of guilt, blame, or shame; or a tension within my body, this decision would not be good.

If my newly developed attitudes and viewpoints expanded this feeling of stillness and endorsed this song of joy, then I would adopt these new postulates, these new thoughts or emotional patterns, and then build upon them. It felt like a rebirth of spirit and produced a tremendous sense of freedom.

Another distinction was born from the stillness within. I would on occasion recite the mantra, "Love at all costs but with boundaries." There is a thin line from having boundaries and being compassionate. It comes from wisdom.

Wisdom comes from being indifferent and allowing Divine Spirit to show a direction outside of the box of social consciousness and in balance within the situation. In that way, I can be detached from the pressures of others and maintain the golden glow of soul.

Through wisdom, I can see the motivation beyond the stories of people. Talk is cheap and illusionary, but facts are real. Sometimes, it is brutal to defend truth in the midst of those who have different agendas. Many times, it is harder to do what is right instead of doing what is easy.

When it is my turn to handle a difficult situation, I take the attitude that my number is up; it is my turn at bat in the most important game of my life. I need to keep my eye on the ball and stay focused on the important task at hand. I must step out of the comfort zone and be indifferent to social consciousness. I must follow the light of spirit and the sound within my spiritual heart and just go for it, with great enthusiasm and zest. I must be courageous.

When it was my turn, I knew that I would take some knocks and blows and stumbles from the spiritually blind and ignorant. That is part of the game. No longer is social acceptance most important. I am in the great escape, the great emancipation to spiritual freedom. Because of my efforts and the grace of God, I was shown intermittent glimpses of the beauty of heaven. That is what kept me going; that is what's important now.

The best part of the indifference lessons are that they allow for the appreciation of the richness of the present moment and the awareness of the knowingness of the right brain. Indifference creates a bridge between the physical and the spiritual. This bridge allows the stillness, love, happiness, and freedom that were continually growing within my heart to be expressed in the physical dimension.

———————

Indifference was the platform of empowerment, which enabled me to develop freedom from the social consciousness, freedom from the morals, and freedom from the ethics as laid down by religions and other political entities.

Remember, the primary objective of politics is to control the masses, to establish its version of law and order, to limit choices. The objective of religion is to establish rules of morality and ethics and also to limit choices. Sometimes, church and state combine their coercive powers and create outlandish dictates to rule the people, with the promise of eternal glory if you obey and eternal damnation and severe corporal punishment if you do not.

Indifference from social consciousness enables me to develop my own codes of morals and ethics built upon the foundation of spiritual consciousness. I must add that my codes of ethics and morality are on a much higher level of integrity than social consciousness. I did not establish a code of ethics without a balance of personal integrity and righteous discrimination.

Discrimination, in my experience, is the combination of turning away from something you do not want while at the same time turning towards a new focus on the things that you do want.

I had to practice constant vigilance on the subtle influences of social consciousness on practically every domain in my life. I had to pay perpetual attention to my body's innate response to expand and drop my shoulders when something was for my good or the tendency to contract and tighten my shoulders when something was bad. This was linked to attention to my spiritual heart's response. I was able to fashion a new Dax. I was able to become more of my unique self with much disregard to others' opinion of me.

When my intent is exempt from the pressures of shoulds and should nots and the norms of social consciousness, I can express this inner song within my spiritual heart. Being still, being present, and being indifferent nullify the worry and anxiety from other peoples' opinions. I try to do my best; I try to find fun and enjoyment and to be the conduit for Divine Spirit under all situations.

Regardless of my endeavor, it is impossible to please everyone. Remember, people can only see me and my intent in situations coming from their state of consciousness, their character, and their agenda. They project their story on to me and declare that that is what I was thinking or feeling and why I took a specific action. In reality, they do not have a clue. This is the large part of social consciousness that I am nullifying by my attitude.

Their opinion of me is not my business because their opinion of me is really who they are and not who I am. They do not have a clue of the depths of my consciousness or the experiences that make me uniquely myself. They can only judge me through their limited social consciousness.

16

MIND AND SOUL

I repeat throughout this book that I am trying to break the habit of the automatic left-brain social consciousness and enter into right-brain spiritual consciousness. I strive for the conscious blending of the right-brain spiritual consciousness with the left-brain social consciousness.

Basically, the mind is an absolutely fabulous machine. It can be trained to do very highly skilled tasks by repetition and by the operator's belief in himself. The hardwired left brain works with the deduction process but has no power to create new concepts. It works primarily by habit, and habit is usually the chief dictator of mental action. The mind loves routine and dislikes changes or new ideas. The mind usually accepts whatever is impressed on it at the early stage of development as truth.

In contrast, the right brain works with the information received from the spiritual senses through the third eye and from the heavenly music residing within your spiritual heart, your song of joy.

The left brain works by evaluating all new experiences and comparing them to all of the knowledge and beliefs stored in the memory banks of the left brain, which I called the filter system. The mind then makes a decision to ensure the perpetuation of the ego.

Information from both the left brain and the right brain then goes to the executive division of the mind for the exact execution of your programming.

Miracles can happen as a result of the intricacies of the mind. The filter system has been temporarily deleted of its belief system, and therefore, it is able to produce something unusual because the usual limitations from the mind filters have been removed. The prime example of this phenomenon is what happens in hypnosis when individuals totally listen to the suggestion of the hypnotist and thereby bypass their filter systems to execute the new commands.

Another way to bypass the filter system is from an influence from a stronger power. Emergencies have created opportunities for miraculous things to happen because the situation dictates the bypass of our filter system. In that situation, impossible can become possible. The mother lifting a car off her child comes to mind.

The mind produces sensations of thought processes because of the thalamus and hypothalamus, part of the brain relationship to the pineal and pituitary glands. Different thought patterns are usually linked to certain emotional patterns that produce different body sensations. This situation is why some people get confused in relationships. They get accustomed to the sensation of anger, control, lust, or vanity and accept that as the norm.

Usually, it is an unchallenged sensation until it is confronted by a higher and stronger emotion like fear, guilt, and shame or by the other end of the spectrum: sensations created by the stillness of spirit. The more a habit is indulged in, the harder it is to break this mold.

The positive feedback of approval is the physical sensation that keeps the belief system alive, as well as the fear of what happens if you decide to rebel.

It is extremely hard to break old habits and customs, especially if they are associated with a long and strong accepted belief system and policed by an even stronger set of rules.

Many church leaders know this fact and create rules and regulations for their members. Christians wrote these rules into the Bible and say that it is the word of God. They make many decisions for their followers that the followers should be making for themselves. The followers give their power away and follow like sheep. There is usually the promise of eternal damnation if you dare think outside of the Bible or challenge authority. Followers like the idea of letting others make their decisions, until the light of soul breaks through their mental prison.

Fortunately (and unfortunately), many religions have many good principles. In my experience with the Catholic church, I had many good experiences following the doctrine of that religion. I was very blessed by being raised a devout Catholic. Similarly, I was extremely blessed when I decided to leave.

My college experience was the advent of my spiritual growth. I knew it was time to do my own thinking and make my own decisions, especially when it came to my relationship with Divine Spirit and spiritual freedom.

The courageous find freedom. Whether it is spiritual freedom, political freedom, or freedom from customs, I was willing to add a greater powerful influence to break free. I was lucky that on the three mentioned occasions, I was forced to look deep within to evaluate the subjective reality created by my beliefs. I decided to keep some beliefs and discard others.

I had a double incentive. I desperately wanted to leave something behind, and I definitely wanted to travel to something much greater. Enlightenment instigated a change of beliefs and habits. These new beliefs and habits helped instigate enlightenment. Then enlightenment instigated more changes. Hence the cycle of growth and enlightenment continued.

The incentive for my decisions was my desire for freedom. My old beliefs did not align with my newly acquired observation of life, which allowed me to experience feelings of expansion and beauty. The peace and joy of this developing spiritual awakening was greater than my desire for the security of my ego and social consciousness. However, cultivated indifference cracked the door that allowed the influence of soul and Divine Spirit into my mind, which started the journey of my spiritual emancipation.

Understanding and knowing the mechanics of the mind enabled me to utilize that information to my advantage. I made it a point to stay aware of the now, to start observing the information received by the spiritual eye and the right brain, and to consciously allow this information to enter the mix in the filter system of my mind.

From the daily spiritual exercise of contemplation, in which I would slip into benediction with Divine Spirit and experience ultimate beauty of the light and essence of the inner heavens, I would distill these experiences into my filter system from the right brain.

I am consciously changing the thoughts and belief patterns in the censor division of my mind to the spiritual viewpoint that I am soul. From that viewpoint, the experiences that the executive division manifests deepen my awareness of the spiritual light and spiritual sound. I know that everything that comes to me through the workings of the mind has to be for my enlightenment and spiritual freedom.

If I consistently put good things into my filter, the executive division has to give me good things in return. Good things sometimes come in strange situations and circumstances. From the spiritual consciousness, is the good really good and the bad really bad? Are the ups really up and downs really down? On the other hand, is that social consciousness determining what is good and what is bad?

There is tremendous peace and contentment that come from a higher perspective. It is peaceful to accept life as it comes, accepting the ups with the downs, the good with the bad, and the ugly with the beautiful, and just keep shining.

The more I surrender into this spiritual current, the more Divine Spirit directs my life into greater spiritual freedom.

17

MIND AND CHANGE

The mind is not the thinker of the thought; soul is responsible for that. Unfortunately, the censor in the brain is programmed by social and religious norms that have a tendency to handicap soul's transmissions. These norms severely limit soul's ability to communicate clearly.

Indifference is a tool that allows me to start paying attention to the now instead of the habitual automatic running of the left brain, which makes decisions based on the past memories. The now opened up for me the opportunity to start becoming aware of the influence of my right brain. This part of my brain integrates into my neurology different information and sensations that are a natural effect of stillness. The spiritual light and spiritual sounds were always there, but I was unaware. I became aware of many different spiritual realities happening simultaneously while living in the physical.

The more I explored and studied the different qualities of vibration coming from the spiritual eye and spiritual heart, the more I became aware of many beautiful things that I have read about in different spiritual books but had never experienced. These other worlds were becoming real.

By making this realization automatic, I was able to counteract the automatic opinion of my social programming. This new habit became a major step in my emancipation.

As I constantly endeavored to practice the disciplines that allowed me to become aware of the higher vibrations of spiritual sensations as they hit my spiritual eye and spiritual heart, some interesting things became central in my awareness.

Many times, I would go in conscious awareness to places that are beyond brain activity. When I returned to physical awareness, I could remember just as much as I could bring back within the availability or possibility of my mind's acceptance. Making mental sense of the inner experiences was quite limiting.

However, the spiritual experience would leave its impact upon my neurology the same way it left the impact of any physical, mental, or emotional experience. Soul imparted onto my physical, mental, emotional, and spiritual self the remembrance of these new spiritual experiences. By becoming aware of the spiritual vibrations from my pineal gland, soul would remember this soul journey by the tone left behind during its travel into this new spiritual environment.

At that period of time, when I started to learn about and experience soul journey, I was very fortunate to meet a renowned spiritual traveler, who protected me and guided me.

The mental concept of following the guidance and protection of my spiritual master is no new idea. I just had to make some alterations within the belief system I already had. Like so many other things that I learned in my childhood, I now had the choice to keep what I believed was true, to discard what I believed was not, or to alternate the beliefs as I spiritually mature.

The next step was to start becoming aware of and to make sense of the new spiritual vibrations that were now available from this fresh new viewpoint of me as soul.

When soul enters the physical form as an infant to start a new life within, it comes in with a huge knowing, but it is very perplexed with all of these new neurological sensations bombarding its brain. It has to make sense of the vibrations that are coming in through his eyes. He does not know what he is seeing, but he knows something is happening. He is being bombarded with sensations coming from his ears, mouth, nose, and touch. He needs to figure out what is going on here. He constantly orientates himself into his physical environment.

He needs to learn how to communicate when he is hungry, when he needs assistance to relieve unpleasant sensations, and when he is happy and content.

He innately knows the sensation of love, fear, anger, joy, and the other emotions and learns how to respond to them to ensure his safety. He gradually becomes stabilized into the physical reality with the understanding of these new vibrations.

Remember that this soul entered this tiny body with the knowing of the heavens that he left to come here. He is automatically orientated into the right brain of knowing the oneness of it all, the knowing of the divine love of God, and the knowing of who he is as soul and his connection with Divine Spirit.

But there comes a time when he forgets his inheritance; he is educated through his left brain into the socialization and into the religious beliefs of his parents or his environment. He forgets because those who teach him have also forgotten.

Even with the greatest and purest intent, we humans seem to have forgotten who we really are and the immense love and beauty that is awaiting us now.

Just as the soul of the new baby needs to be orientated into its new environment, I had to be reorientated back into the environment of soul from which I came. I needed different tools and different disciplines to start making sense of the new vibrations and their realities that I was receiving. When soul journeying beyond the mind, I was dealing with a completely new set of rules, a wholly new set of vibrations to make sense of and to interpret. I was learning the new foreign language of spiritual reality.

The pineal gland, pituitary gland, thalamus, and hypothalamus, sometimes collectively referred to as the crystal palace, along with the right-brain input and the spiritual heart connection, needed to be developed and nourished.

18

THE PHYSICAL AND EMOTIONAL

I will attempt to explain this new way of living, this new way of being from the awareness of these new vibrations, this new way of knowing or thinking, as soul using the mind as an instrument to anchor itself into the physical reality.

In order for me to grasp with my intellect what I was experiencing with the new vibrations coming through my third eye and spiritual heart, I referenced these experiences with a small number of books that resonated with me. These books resonated with me because they were written by knowledgeable spiritual travelers.

A spiritual traveler is an extremely highly developed spiritual being whose mission is to assist soul in becoming proficient with the vibrations of the spiritual planes revealed to the neophyte during the soul journey. His job is to help soul become proficient with these new energies that lead to the great emancipation.

As I became aware of these new spiritual realities, I also became aware of the presence of the spiritual traveler. I came to love the spiritual traveler and came to respect, honor, and appreciate his magnificent beauty and powerful presence. I love this beautiful being because I cannot help it. The love the spiritual traveler showers on me cannot be denied or ignored. I can only reciprocate the love to my maximum capacity. His job is his joy, and that is to guide and protect me during my spiritual emancipation.

Most of the information these spiritual travelers shared had very similar viewpoints, but they approach the subject from different angles. These various concepts allowed me to form a mental picture from my own experiences by applying the intellectual knowledge presented.

The spiritual travelers had a consensus about how these inner heavens are constructed. There is a cosmology of heaven. They were also in agreement that the kingdom of heaven is within; to recognize this was to know oneself as soul. They also had an agreement that soul journey was the quickest way to this realization and to emancipation.

There is an understanding that there are many layers or planes of heaven. Each plane is composed of the mixture of the positive polarity of spirit with the negative polarity composed of matter, energy, space, and time.

As soul goes higher into these different layers of heaven, there is a change in the mixture of more positive polarity than negative polarity. The more positive polarity that a particular layer of heaven has, the greater the light, sound, or spiritual essence becomes and the more freedom soul has from the negative polarity.

The more positive polarity that exists in these heavens, the longer the life span is in that region and the more freedom soul obtains. It is easier and quicker to manifest because of the increased spiritual powers obtained in those different regions.

There is a place in one of the higher heavenly planes beautifully described by St. John in the Christian Bible and by other saints in their spiritual writings. It is in this heaven where there are roads paved with gold; palaces appear to be made of pearls, with roofs and awnings covered with jewels, studded with emeralds and diamonds and flowers made of jewels as well. The people there are very beautiful in character and live in a high degree of joy. Their life spans are for hundreds of thousands of years; that gives the impression of immortality.

Even though it is known as a very high heaven of universal mind consciousness, sometimes referred to as Christ consciousness, there is a degree of negative polarity that exists therein. A few higher heavens have even less negative polarity. Then there are the heavens of pure positive polarity.

I became aware of these different layers of heaven by becoming aware of the mixture of polarity that exists within that region.

The Physical Heaven

In the physical reality, I am aware that I am here because of the sensations that I am picking up from my five senses. My eyes, ears, nose, taste, and skin sensation make up the normal human sense experience. The vibrations from the sense organs go to my brain, and I interpret physical reality from them. These instruments allow me to realize the physical and to use while I am here. I came to appreciate the magnificent beauty and function of these spectacular instruments and their experience. I came to appreciate physical reality even more by the integration of spiritual awareness.

If you would remember after I left Oklahoma, I was living in the country in Little Paris, Missouri. I dedicated quite a bit of my time and energy into the discovery of the spiritual realities within and beyond the physical, mental, and emotional realms. I became aware of many new and subtle energy domains that paralleled the development of my new spiritual insights. I was also led to the study of new and different energy systems of acupuncture not presented in the traditional acupuncture curriculum. Together with these investigations, I became aware of the chakra system.

Briefly, there are seven chakras. Each chakra relates to different aspects of the physical, emotional, psychological, and spiritual aspects of our lives. Each individual chakra is where specific emotional, psychological, and spiritual needs meet the physical expression. Each chakra is directly connected to the acupuncture system and to the nervous system. If a need is not met, it will cause a tension, a contraction, a decrease of the flow of chi (spirit) to the end organ related to the acupuncture or nervous system. It could also manifest in the expression of negative emotions, and psychological and spiritual qualities.

For example, the third chakra is physically associated with the digestive system. Psychologically, it is related to the expression and development of your unique individuality and ego. It is the gut feeling that helps make decisions. Spiritually, it is connected with the expression of your will, to be yourself and the responsibility to make your own choices as what is best for your autonomy.

The expression of a healthy third chakra is hampered by the emotions of guilt, blame, and shame. Those emotions are used to control or limit your choices and are the foundation of religious consciousness, which uses fear to control social consciousness.

By becoming aware of both the positive and negative subtle energies of the chakras and their relationship to a happy and joyful expression of the flow of spirit through my physical body, I was able to make choices that expanded my spiritual heart to give and receive more of Divine Spirit's blessings. The physical became enhanced and more luminous.

I became more appreciative of the bodily sensations. These physical sensations were placed in a new pecking order of importance. I live in the knowing that I am soul, and I have a body. I can allow the full experience of the sensations and physical expressions by being in the now, free from the guilt, blame, and shame of my religious upbringing.

Once I became aware that I am soul having a Dax experience and in control of the story I create from my bodily sensations, I was able to put the physical sensations in a balanced position. Then I became aware that the next step for me was to realize that I am not my emotions, either.

Emotions are like physical sensations; they are automatic, and for the most part, we are taught which ones are good and which ones are bad. Emotions are links to the physical form through the thalamus and hypothalamus, located near the center of the brain. They create sensations from the emotions and integrate them into the physical body. People come to like some of them and dislike others, depending on the feedback they get from the environment.

There is an array of different emotions. Some become classified as negative, which means they contract, choke, limit, and restrict action and do not allow the free flow of spirit. In my experience, the higher or more positive the emotion, the more I feel expansive; the more freedom I have to express myself, the easier it is to breathe, and the easier it is to move the body and to be joyful.

My observation is dropping the shoulders and trusting in Spirit seems to be the primary ingredients of the positive emotions. On the opposite end, I have observed that fear and ignorance seem to be the primary ingredients of the negative emotions. I have observed that the more negative an emotion is classified, the more of a sense of fear it has. Social approval, control, and security of the ego are a common element of fear. How did I release them?

Emotional freedom started with the awareness that they did, in fact, control me. Other people's opinions of me definitely influenced me. I was forced to release social approval, control, and security of the ego, because they proved to be false gods that I depended upon to bring truth, justice, and integrity into my life.

Again, the way that I enjoyed the experience of the higher, more joyful emotions in a balanced way was to be in tune with something that allowed me a greater sense of fulfillment and enjoyment. Again, it was found by paying attention to the now, paying attention to the higher spiritual vibrations and beauty within each emotion, paying attention to the spiritual light and essence that accompany each different emotion; the spiritual freedom that comes with it freed me to choose the most positive emotion to match the individual circumstance.

When I was a neophyte, learning the discipline of observing my emotions and then choosing whether I wanted to keep it or replace it with a positive one, I had this remarkable emotional epiphany:

I thought I was going to die in the next three hours, so what was really important now that death was knocking at my door? The physical, social, and monetary statuses became completely irrelevant. People's opinion of me or my opinion of them had no significance, no importance. I was compelled to forgive anybody and everybody for anything and everything. Everything that happened in the past was totally unreal, only a memory.

I was stripped of everything. Thoughts and emotions were irrelevant. What is real, significant, important at a time like this? Even time became another unreal illusion. What was left? There was nothing of any material importance left. Everything was gone. I was absolutely alone. What showed up?

The perfection, the totality of the now appeared. This now existed in infinity. It had everything in it, yet at the same time, it was a void, a nothingness. The only thing that existed was this monumental vibration of love. It presented to me a unique sensation of the immensity and infinite vastness of spiritual freedom.

This is who I am. I am a drop within this ocean of love and mercy that has everything within it and exists everywhere. I am sustained by it. I am a manifestation of it. It is the essence of all of the spiritual universes, including the physical.

That experience put a titanic perspective to being indifferent to emotions. They are not me, and I can choose which emotion I want to indulge in. The whole gamut of emotions still automatically happen, since the left brain is still operating. Because I am still living in the human form, the social consciousness will be there. However, I can be in this world, not of it. I can choose, and I do choose the emotion of eternity. I choose the now.

The emotion of the now instills within me a state of peace, stillness, and spiritual love. Within that space is that monumental vibration of the light, sound, or spiritual essence of Divine Spirit that puts me in harmony with all things. It is that inner tone, that melody of Divine Spirit, the flow of the word through soul. This powerful force allows me to be indifferent to others and to give them goodwill. This magnificent tone allows me to give deep friendship to some and even a deeper spiritual love to only a few.

From my academic homework, I have found there are numerous concepts indicating that it is of ultimate importance to manage the emotional state. It is from the emotional state that subjective reality is constructed by the story invented regarding the observed objective experience. Since most people construct their imaginary story based on a mélange of emotions and social consciousness experiences, they end up getting a multitude of stories based on the interest, knowledge, purpose, and agenda of the observer.

Since I have disciplined myself to be indifferent, to consciously attempt to keep my focus on the emotions of the now, and to start observing my socially created stories of my observations, I am able to reinvent my subjective reality into a story that is expansive, fun, and free.

The primary purpose of knowingly living my life free from this illusion is to stay connected to the higher vibrations coming from my third eye and to stay connected to the melodies of heaven in my spiritual heart. My near-death experience totally changed my concept of what is important.

The next level of the spiritual planes for me to explore was the vibrations of the mind worlds. This level of heaven is what the aforementioned St. John and a few other spiritual saints and travelers wrote about. They declare this heaven as the ultimate heaven of most of the earthly religions.

19

KNOWLEDGE VERSUS KNOWING

In the last chapter, I presented my near-death experience and the understanding of how indifference and academic synthesizing has led me to restructure my approach to emotions. Now I will try to explain my new approach to the mental dimensions.

The art and science of the soul journey was the spiritual exercise that made it possible for me to become aware of the higher vibrations, where the higher levels of light and spiritual sound and joy and bliss exist. As I became aware of the existence of these higher vibrations and became familiar with them, I realized that I am soul having a Dax experience. When I changed my subjective viewpoint on reality from the ego to soul, it initiated many physical, emotional, and mental changes that led eventually to spiritual emancipation.

When I do a soul journey spiritual exercise, I often go into places within the inner self to a place of immeasurable stillness and beauty. It is here that I experienced this bliss, which is difficult to describe with language. Trying to describe it or even put it into a mental concept is impractical because of the vastness involved;

the light and spiritual essence there are so immense that only soul can comprehend. The mind cannot encompass or contained it.

That is why I know that logic and knowledge are from the mental worlds, and knowing and intuition are from a higher level than the mind. Knowing and intuition is an art and science developed with awareness, attention, study, and practice.

Have you ever looked at one of those pictures where everything looks blurry and really does not look like a picture at all? However, if you stare at it long enough, suddenly a three-dimensional picture appears. I invite you to start observing that when you see an object, for example a tree, pay more attention to the space in which the tree shows up than the tree itself. When you hear something, pay more attention to the silence in which the sound shows up. This will help you to change your subjective viewpoint.

The mind is a very powerful instrument. I take for granted the many miracles that it produces for me daily and automatically; for the most part, I was entirely unaware. The mind is a magnificent instrument with many functions. I will only cover a few primary functions related to my emancipation experience.

While I started looking at how the mind creates things from the vibrations of my sense organs and from the sensations of my hormonal system and energetic systems, I saw the picture like those weird picture puzzles mentioned in the above paragraph. Abruptly, an image appears; there it is. I came to realize that space, time, and physical substance are not real. They are actually mental constructs that are created within my mind. For me, this is a phenomenal occurrence that I gave no thought to because it came so natural. I learned to accept this marvel without question.

When I see a tree, I am seeing the end results of the vibrations from that tree hitting my eyes and from the chemical and neurological functions stimulating a part of my brain in which I have learned to interpret as a tree.

Do we all see the same tree? In my opinion, what we see is relative to our perception, and to our various interests, purpose, and agenda. Does a logger see the same tree as a tourist? It depends upon the story created in the mind of the observer. All observers live in their own imaginary world created by their stories.

When I see an image from my spiritual eye, I am seeing the result of the vibrations of that image and from the chemical and neurological functions stimulating a different part of my brain than my physical senses. I learned to interpret what I see from my spiritual senses.

The problem I had was that I had to readjust my socialized belief system to what my brain was seeing and interpreting. What I was observing in my new awareness of the spiritual vibrations was as real to me as the tree is in my physical vibrations. Initially, there was no logical or reasonable explanation to explain my observations. Rather, there was a tendency to go for more denial than to offer explanation.

As I soul journey to another heavenly plane in the spiritual realities, I attuned to a completely different set of vibrations. The vibrations are of a finer quality, which means they are more positive and less negative, and I have to readjust to learn to interpret what I am observing in this new area. I have to become familiar with and accustomed to this higher level of vibration, just as a newborn baby must become familiar with the new vibrations of the physical.

There is huge amount of knowledge acquired by experiencing the spiritual realities by soul journey. The experience, for most people, supersedes the socialized educational paradigms. I speculated whether the establishment mentioned in the previous chapters did not know any better, or did they hide the truth because they would loosen their control over me? Perhaps it was a little bit of both. For me, this was the beginning of a new concept to explore: the difference between knowing and knowledge.

Previously, I explained how the mind works, how there is the gathering of vibrations or experiences which go through our filter systems of knowledge and beliefs, which we interpret for the purpose of the survival of the ego. Then this decision goes to the executive division for execution.

Our belief system changes as we discover and exchange for a better belief than the one we had. The new paradigms can either expand you and allow more freedom or contract you to limit your expression.

As mentioned earlier, I had three negative experiences of social injustice that made me realize that my old belief system was riddled with major flaws, and I desperately needed change. That was my incentive.

The other initiator of change was allowing input from the right-brain evaluation and interpretation, along with constant attention to the now and to the love experience by the light and spiritual sound during soul journey. Because of these inputs, there were major shifts made to my belief system towards the spiritual instead of the social.

One magnificent tool that allowed a major spiritual shift to elevate my spiritual beliefs to supersede my educational knowledge was the use of intuition. Intuition is the power of knowing instead of knowledge. Intuition is the power of knowing without the input from the physical, emotional, or mental faculties. It is the ability to know without the interference of the intelligence or reasoning. It is an innate human talent where I can get spiritual guidance, instructions, and knowledge from a higher source than the mind, through my reality as soul.

From my experience, indifference and stillness are two of the starting blocks for intuition. They set the stage for neutrality, where the most correct answer to the situation can show up. Because I am working with a tool that is beyond the matrix of the mind, I had to learn new disciplines to access this knowingness.

Indifference and stillness are qualities used by soul to link intuition or knowing to the mind and to knowledge. The trick is to balance knowing and the mind together as a team, but making sure that intuition stays the quarterback. The quarterback needs the rest of the team to be successful, especially in the physical world. Even though intuition will know the answer, I had to implement the action through the mind suited to the given circumstances.

The integration of intuition with the mind is a learned habit. The more I used it, the easier it became to use intuited information or knowing in my decisions. Intuition is always available to me. I just had to train myself to pay attention and to create a channel for it to flow into my awareness. I had to learn to trust it and to overcome the unique and subtle fears that accompanied the integration of anything new.

Intuition has information that cannot be gained from any amount of education, created knowledge, or fabricated logic or reasoning. Predominantly because intuition does not use words, it uses impressions. It is one of those higher vibrations that I had to train myself to become familiar with and then use.

When I stopped trying to translate my impressions into left-brain language and familiarity and started focusing on using the right-brain language and its imagination ability, I started to excel in understanding intuitive impressions from the higher spiritual worlds. It was like immersing myself in a foreign country to learn the language. Very quickly, the knowing of the new language becomes automatic. I had to stop thinking in English and start using the spiritual language. Once I did that, I could then begin to translate the spiritual language into understanding with the left brain and integrate it into my subjective story.

The training of integrating intuitive knowledge with mind knowledge is a talent that can be developed into a high degree of success. The energy and effort expended to do this brought delight and fun into my life because of the naturally right guidance that I got from my higher self. It took (and still takes) trial-and-error experiment to constantly upgrade and adjust my proficiency. I had to work through many obstacles and aberrations that prevented the balanced integration of intuition with knowledge.

Besides guidance and increase enjoyment of the physical, mental, and emotional aspects of my life, there is another plus factor for spiritual enlightenment: By developing the sense of knowing, which operates above the mind, I was developing a talent to use in my soul journey experiences.

I was so used to using the mind knowledge to operate in physical, mental, and emotional domains that I had to get used to the concept of knowing without the mind. I had to get used to the idea of obtaining information in the absence of all thought. I had to get used to the idea of seeing and hearing and becoming aware of myself as soul without using the mental faculties of seeing and hearing to become aware of where I was. I was learning this new foreign language of the soul journey.

I was so used to creating by using the mind to manifest my existence in space and time and to manifest my realities in the physical, mental, and emotional vibrations that it was tough to learn the next discipline. How does one manifest without the mind?

20

IMAGINATION
PART 1

From my mystical experience, blended with academic reading of spiritual travelers, I will consolidate my perspective of soul. It will be a very condensed perspective.

God created soul, a tiny spark of itself, and then sent soul into the worlds of polarity so it can have experiences until it becomes aware that it is this spark of Divine Love.

Soul, this ball of light and consciousness, upon awakening to its true identity on a place like planet Earth, has to be orientated to a new set of realities. One reality that it has to adapt to is its true nature as soul, and the other reality is of soul having a human experience.

The mind is the most powerful tool we have but imagination is the greatest spiritual gift God has given to all of its creation. It is the most important because we create all of our realities from the use of this gift. Imagination along with language molds our physical, emotional, mental and spiritual stories that manifest our realities.

The second most important gift we received through the growth and development of imagination is that we are soul and have a body, emotions, beliefs and an ego to create experiences to teach us how to love and how to be free.

However, once soul has touched the fabric of God's powerful spiritual love through Divine Spirit, we use this gift to gain emancipation from salvation. Soul forsakes all of his social programming to meld into the Sacred Heart of God. The awakening of soul by the fire of the Holy Spirit and the song of the Word compels soul to journey deeper into the vortex of Divine Spirit. Spirituality is caught; it is not taught.

The soul journey that awaits you as soul is beyond words and is uniquely yours. Spirit will customize your path so that you can develop your unique and special gifts and talents. Imagination and soul realization are the keys that make this development possible. Part of your emancipation is developing your individuality. It is difficult to do this if someone else controls your imagination.

It is imperative to develop conscious awareness to the use of imagination. Be on guard to the subtle and not-so-subtle organizations, entities, or people who want to steal, control, or limit your imagination. The advertising industry is a prime example. Some religious groups and some social organizations are other examples.

Emotions are another subtle influence that can cast a spell on and capture the imagination. Emotions have always used the imagination to play out difficult circumstances in order to satisfy the ego and social consciousness. An example is the emotion of revenge. We have a way of settling matters with the imagination in which we get even or always get the upper hand.

Instead of reaction in social consciousness by imagining sweet revenge and thereby losing the connection to Divine Spirit, we can regain the presence by imagining responding in a calm manner and with a spiritual viewpoint. Leave revenge to the higher power that knows all the variables and can balance the karma of the incident quicker and more effectively (some of that karma may be your own).

Imagine responding to life from a higher spiritual point of view, centered in the flow of Divine Spirit through the spiritual heart. Learn to trust and to follow the guidance of the whisper of Divine Spirit within your spiritual heart. There is more wisdom inside your spiritual heart than in any book.

Logic and knowledge can only help explain what is happening. Once you have had the experience of soul realization and have received the kiss of love from Divine Spirit, you will understand your compassion for those who try to find emancipation through reading and logic. You can understand their awareness by the story they relate.

Books and academics are only tools to set the ambience of your emotions to the state of stillness and holiness. These states are usually the launch pad to soul journey. It is the spiritual light and sound or essence that is your teacher and the tools that impart wisdom into your sacred heart, which becomes your guiding influence.

This light and sound and the presence of your master resides within your sacred heart, within the seat of soul, not within your head. Soul's connection to God is through knowing; man's connection to God is through knowledge.

I am soul having a human experience. In my reality, it is the blend of both knowing with knowledge that directs my intent. But I always attempt to keep love, wisdom, and the freedom of knowing from soul's connection to Divine Spirit paramount and the first priority.

The true adventure of this experience comes from the fluctuation of the intensity of my consciousness in being totally present. This means being totally here and totally in the now where this connection with Divine Spirit is unhampered and the blend of knowing and knowledge is balanced.

I say "intensity" because sometimes the impact of something negative or something unjust attacks and attaches to my spirit, and I spiral downward with the pull of the ego. I temporarily lose my indifferent and objective viewpoint.

That's okay because I am having a human experience, and sometimes, it's overwhelming. I attempt to calibrate myself back to stillness, peace, and the smile energy by changing my subjective story, by finding the silver lining in the dark cloud. I ask my spiritual traveler and the healing angels to assist me in detaching the negative energy and in healing the nonphysical wound.

Sometimes, I do it quickly, and sometimes, it takes a while to reorientate myself into the knowing that all is being taking care of by the love and grace of Divine Spirit. My quest is to stay on the path of love.

I came to realize that my commitment, my earnest desire is to meld deeper into the sacred heart of my beloved Divine Spirit. This request allows spirit to send me experiences that teach me what part of my ego or social consciousness I need to release to become more indifferent in order to gain more spiritual freedom and to experience more of the rapture of the kiss of the Divine Love. I subjectively trust that what Spirit brings to me is for my spiritual growth and part of God's perfect plan.

Interestingly, I discovered that I need to become indifferent to both the good as well as the bad experiences. I cannot hold on to either, or it will negate the intensity of the here and the now experience.

Soul reality is so different from what I was taught by the religious doctrine in my childhood. When I started to become aware of what it means, it was an addition of new perspectives as well as a replacement of my old ideals.

Thoughts, emotions, beliefs, and the physical are not part of soul reality. It is a whole different reality in which the physical, emotions, and beliefs are instruments used to express the flow of Divine Spirit through me. They are not me.

Heaven is not necessarily a place but more of a state of awareness of this flow. This state could be of the here and now in the region of space, time, energy, and matter. It could be in a heaven of the universal mind consciousness or a heaven in the spiritual nothing/everything consciousness.

The heavens of my ideal are beyond the mental and emotional aspects. They are influenced by soul reality. I endeavor to become detached from the vanity of my mental and emotional beliefs in order to dwell deeper into spiritual realities and soul reality.

When I die, I will go to a region in the nonphysical heavens. It can only be at that place that matches soul's relationship to spirit. Regardless of what heavenly region I will dwell in, I can only take the love in my heart and the spiritual consciousness I have developed.

21

IMAGINATION
PART 2

I am not sure if it was my experience with imagination, supplemented by my academic research into the subject, or if it was my academic research that added substance to my experience. I suspect it is a combination of both approaches that opened the door to make sense of the two aspects of imagination I am about to present. Each aspect of imagination was very significant for my spiritual emancipation.

The first aspect is how to build a world of reality in the higher heavens above the vibrations of the mind worlds, when there is no mind. We are so accustomed to the mechanics of the mind and the use of the laws of the universal mind consciousness, which seem so automatic, that we overlook the physiology on how the laws work here in the physical. In the physical, emotional, and mental vibration or planes, the mind is the primary instrument of manifestation or creation. How does imagination fit in?

The second aspect is how to use the imagination I developed in the higher heavenly vibration and apply it to manifesting my world in the physical.

When I am working in a dimension that is without a mind, which means there is no time or space or cause-and-effect, it is perplexing until I become familiar with different and new concepts of abstracts to practice. I have to work with a new dimension of relativity.

The key to my understanding of the use of imagination in spirituality, to see, visualize, and be in the higher worlds, all starts with the continual awareness of the now that allows for a new state of consciousness. This is the initial step to interpret the vibrations that are received from soul to create a reality.

Staying attuned to the now is a very hard thing to do while living in the physical, mental, and emotional realities. The lures of social consciousness had me so trained to worry about the past and the future that those anxieties had me overlooking the now. I had to consciously train myself to stay focused in the now.

The primary discipline to help me focus into the now was to first become aware of the constant anxiety of the mind and then to become indifferent to this chatter. I needed to learn how to quiet the unnecessary noise, to be still, and to observe the novelty of it all.

I started to pay attention to what I was thinking when I was not aware that I was thinking. It was a huge awakening to how unconscious I was at times and how I ran on automatic social consciousness. I had to make a conscious effort to offset the negative unconscious and automatic thoughts and emotions whenever I lost focus of the now. The discipline I learned was to habitually and consciously start thinking thoughts that made me happy and expansive.

What also helps me to orientate myself physically into the now is by paying attention to my body. I focus on my breathing; I focus on releasing stress that I may have in my organs, like my stomach or heart, or in my pelvic floor. I focus on relaxing my muscles, especially the muscles in my face, in my shoulders, and around my spine.

Additionally, I pay attention to what I am seeing. I start observing textures, shapes, and people. I start paying attention to what I am hearing and what I am feeling inside. I also focus on the impressions I am receiving from my spiritual eye and spiritual heart. I start to observe my world in wonderment.

Finally, most importantly, I focus on the most enjoyable, fun-loving, and happy thoughts that I can possibly think of in that moment. I allow my imagination to run free. I release anything that is stressful.

What I observed in the now was the perpetual motion of the creative aspects of Divine Spirit. This constant stream of creativity has to be present for anything to exist. Everything is created out of the fabric of spirit that is composed of the light and spiritual essence of God.

For example, a flower is the expression of Divine Spirit as a flower. When I was stuck in social consciousness, I would look at the flower and not really see the flower. However, when I was in the now consciousness, I would observe the flower and notice many qualities and distinctions about its uniqueness and beauty that would expand my heart. I would then create my own story about the flower. Wonderfully, this new story flooded my consciousness, not my worry about the past or anxiety about the future.

From time to time, the mental images or impressions that I would receive from this new spiritual dimension allowed me to make mental sense of them. Then at other times, the logic would totally elude me. Nevertheless, the mental exercise was to be aware that the time was always now and the place was always here. The mental explanation is not as important as the experience.

I progressively made the shift that opened a completely new world of reality for me. I learned the art and science of utilizing my right brain and how to interpret the vibrations from my third eye and my spiritual heart to become sensitive to the melodies of heaven within the stillness.

In order to help me be acquainted with these new realities, I would very slowly read books by selected authors. I would soul journey, in imagination and in consciousness, to the places they described. As the authors were describing the images of the surroundings, I would imagine myself being there.

Progressing from the exercises of being in the now in the physical realities, I would do the same exercises in these spiritual realities. I learned to pay attention to the textures, colors, and qualities of the spiritual environment and the surroundings.

In order to help anchor my imagination in this new spiritual environment, I would create by imagining the people of that region to have forms similar to the human forms I am familiar with and then to interact with them. I realized that the beautiful beings that inhabit this region would appear and manifest in the form of my imagination to jump-start and assist my continuous imagining. We would start our interactions from that place. Then other beings from that region would appear in the experience and interact with me. As our interactions deepened, the clarity of the surroundings brightened, and everything became more genuine, more real.

One thing that stays with me, beside the images of the soul journey experience, is the magnificence of the beauty of the beings and surroundings. However, of equal importance is the quality of the light of that plane and the rapture of the heavenly music that permeates my soul when I am there.

Most of my spiritual experiences happen during my spiritual exercises, when I set a specific time to do my spiritual prayers and my soul journey contemplations. Other times, these spiritual experiences just seem to happen spontaneously. The main common denominator to these unexpected spiritual journeys is I am usually in a space of peace and stillness, and I have a happy heart and happy thoughts.

In the soul journey contemplation, I usually begin by sitting in a chair in the upright position. I make a conscious effort of releasing all stress and tension throughout my whole body. I start with my feet and end with my skin and the top of my head. I then focus on relaxing my thoughts, then totally dropping my shoulders, relaxing my spine, and sensing the subtle but powerful flow of Divine Spirit through the energetic channels of my spine.

As soon as I put the interruptions from the physical to bed and open my spiritual channels to receive the spiritual current, I then focus attention on the impressions from my spiritual eye and from the crown chakra on the top of my head. I then chant a spiritual mantra for a short time. The journey is about to begin. The only thing that I am aware of at this time is my occasional necessity to breathe.

From this very still state, a number of different things can happen; I will comment only on my two favorites. These two types of soul journey experiences have a similar beginning. The one that produces the most memorable experiences but happens less frequently is what I call the awakened dream.

Right before I fall asleep, there is a short blip in time from being awake to falling asleep. In that small period, I capture the moment (or the moment captures me), and I become totally emerged into and conscious of my dream. However, I am not asleep. The experiences at that time are phenomenal and leave an everlasting impression on the knowing that I am soul and that this spiritual experience is real.

Next is another example that fits in the category of the above-mentioned blip spiritual experience. It is different yet similar. I have talked to a few people who have died in the hospital setting and had an out-of-body experience (OBE), then had to return to their physical bodies to fulfill their spiritual destiny or to finish their agreement with Divine Spirit for being here.

These people were dramatically changed by this experience. All of them expressed the effects of this spiritual experience in different ways, but all had a few similar characteristics. They all walked away with the spiritual enlightenment in which they realize that they are soul and not their bodies. All of these individuals reported that they were in a spiritual body, looking down at their physical body that lay on the operating table.

All of these people had a knowing about death which manifested in a deep level of contentment. There was a humble and a peaceful demeanor. All the commotion about death and salvation was of no concern to them, like, "I have been there, done that, now on to bigger and better things, like the joys of life instead of the fear of death."

My most frequent soul journey experience I call the blue light journey. It is a different spiritual sensation than the blip, for I find myself gently gliding through the inner spiritual worlds. It sometimes feels like gliding through outer space, being escorted and accompanied within a blue light of total acceptance and unconditional love.

This gentle gliding has many different forms than the one mentioned above, and experiences last for different durations. The gliding usually comes to a halt in a region of immense beauty and vastness. This was the typical experience that I had when I was a child after Holy Communion in the Catholic faith and during the Benediction ceremony. I would go to these beautiful regions, following the blue light.

Now when I soul journey to these magnificent and beautiful places, I use my imagination and spiritual academics to create many meaningful spiritual experiences. One thing that commonly happens during these journeys is that I get an intuitive impression to bring back with me. To receive the gift of these intuitive impressions is worth the journey; however, there is so much more offered in the spiritual domain.

By blending the academics of my spiritual readings with the art of imagining, I was able to visit many places in the heavenly worlds. Continuous imagining became a natural progression once I was able to free my subjective self from social consciousness and adopt the "I am soul consciousness."

I would like to offer two more of the many available experiences of the use of the imagination. I hope many of you can identify with this next example. When my grandmother was preparing to leave the physical reality and was closing in on her time of departure, she would have conversations with Papa and a few of her close friends, who were already deceased.

My grandmother was already indifferent to many things that once were important to her. Her attention was definitely not about anything in the material but more on her preparation to move on to a different spiritual reality, to the place we go to after death. There were intermittent times when she was her old self and was the Grandma we knew when we were growing up. Yet most of the time, she was preoccupied with other things and had a faraway look in her eyes.

The most interesting things about her conversations with Papa and her two dear friends who had already departed is that they were logical and coherent. She was having a conversation with them as if they were present in the physical. My subjective story is that they were present and were as real to Grandma as Grandma was to me in the physical.

They were real to her because her attention, her orientation into the new dimension where she would be going after death was being prepared. She was innately using soul journey the way

I consciously used soul journey, and for the same purpose: to become aware of the spiritual realities beyond the physical senses.

Since then, I have had conversations with departed people, and they were as real to me from their spiritual reality as they were when we had conversations in the physical reality. This is not that unusual, for I have spoken with many people who have had similar experiences.

You might say that I just have an overdeveloped imagination, and I must agree with you. However, in the physical reality, I am not only inventing the image of a tree in my mind from the vibrations of the tree. I am also inventing the space and the time for the tree to show up. I am using imagination to manifest reality in the physical, the same way I am using imagination to manifest reality in the spiritual planes.

My subjective reality, the interpretation of these spiritual experiences from my spiritual senses, is as real to me as my interpretation of physical reality. They are just interpretations of different vibrational frequencies.

I have observed from this new dimension of soul reality that things work differently above the mind, above space and time. One primary difference is, since I do not have to go anywhere, the way I make things happen is to start imagining I am there. I start visualizing from the impressions I receive, then I and the imagined visualization meld, grow, and develop. I actually imagine what I want, and what I imagine manifests to me instead of me going out to it, as in the physical.

The second thing that I realized from the new dimension and perspective of soul reality versus physical reality is that soul can exist in many worlds at once. The combination of these two aspects of soul reality sets the stage for the second half of this discourse. How do I use imagination that I developed in the higher heavens' vibration and apply it to manifesting my world in the physical?

The Second Aspect

How do I move on to the second aspect of imagination; that is, how do I use imagination from what I experience in the higher heavens' vibration and apply it to manifesting my world in the physical?

Keep in mind that I said that besides the magnificence of the beauty of the beings and surroundings, of equal importance is the quality of the light of that plane and the rapture of the heavenly music that permeates soul when I am there.

There are times when I soul journey to these spiritual regions of heaven, the blue light journey, to bathe in the spiritual current in that domain. Just to see the heavenly lights and to listen and sense with my spiritual heart the heavenly music and essence that exists there is worth the effort.

I anchor my imagination into this region of non-thought. From this place of stillness, indifference, beauty, freedom, power of being, vastness, expansiveness, beyond the mind to the limitless, I do my best to do my thinking and subjectively create my physical, mental, and emotional reality from this region of spiritual consciousness.

Heaven is a state of consciousness, not necessarily a place. It is the state from which I create my subjective reality. The subjective stories determine the world in which I live. When I use creative visualization from that state of beauty, I tend to create and attract into my life situations and people who reflect my projected attitude. This space is so blissful that it supersedes any physical, mental, or emotional rewards gained through social consciousness to satisfy the ego.

I realized the purpose of my many pursuits in life was to make me happy. To be the healer extraordinaire made me proud and was very appealing to my ego. Nevertheless, when it was taken away and declared evil, I realized that social consciousness was lacking. Something was wrong. My attachment to social consciousness, and to people's opinions that had been based on social consciousness, caused me grief. I was allowing the effect to make me either happy or unhappy. I became aware that I had it backwards. I was the effect, not the cause.

I realized that I could be happy because I imagined myself to be and for no apparent reason. Because of this attitude, I attracted new events into my life to complement my state. I created my subjective reality to be a positive, happy story from my place of beauty. I endeavored to stay anchored into this place of beauty regardless of other people's social consciousness or their projections onto me of their states of awareness.

Since I have a body, a mind, and emotions, there are limitations. They are the layers that this spiritual current must flow through to be expressed. These layers, by their very nature, set up limitations to restrict or clog the conduit. However, I endeavor to discipline myself in order to minimize the constrictions. That is why it is important to do contemplative prayer, to soul journey to these high states, on a daily basis to stay anchored into them.

There are constant reminders that soul is in enemy country and will meet resistance in many forms. From my experience, the primary deterrent is that many people are stuck in social consciousness, and social consciousness itself perpetuates the ego.

There was, there is, and there will be judgments and opinions projected onto me by those who are stuck in materiality or social consciousness. They are stuck there through laziness, lack of awareness, or fear of change, or because they like the temporal payoff.

All actions flow from a person's character. If you want to find out the true character of people, put them in positions of authority. Who they really are will come forward. Either they will project their opinions, their subjective story, which is really who they are, on to others and claim that that is who they are. Or they will view the situation from a detached and still attitude, thereby able to see the whole picture and judge from wisdom.

I have noticed that people who are stuck in social consciousness hold others to a higher degree of excellence or ethics than they do themselves. They project their limitations onto others so they do not have to take responsibility and admit that they also have limitations. They live in denial that they are anything less than perfect. They have to be right and are usually are the first to interject negative criticism onto the action and opinions of others. This is usually an expression of fear.

It takes a conscious effort to create a mental habit to be indifferent to the constant onslaught of negativity and stay true to spiritual awareness. This got easier to do as I became increasingly aware of the higher spiritual realities. The heavenly essence and the light from these inner spiritual planes are as real to me as this physical plane. The experiences in these spiritual vibrations make it easier to stay anchored there and easier to dodge or repel ego-based negativity.

By developing imagination, I can find happiness by the inner movement of my consciousness to the most beautiful places I can imagine and from there create my subjective story.

From my experience, imagination is enhanced by adding the use of the impressions from the third eye that are interpreted by the right brain. If you would remember, this information is also added to the mind filter system along with indifference, creative imagining, and creative visualization. This information is then sent to the executive division of the mind, which attracts situations and events into my physical reality to parallel my state of being.

I attempt to manifest the beauty of this inner heavenly essence and shining light into my life by imagining me living in this region while operating a physical, mental, and emotional body. I endeavor to be still, to stay in the moment, in the now, to recognize the beauty of it that I would have ordinarily missed.

I create my subjective stories from indifference. I create them from the wisdom of stillness and by attunement to the vortex, the connection to the flow of spirit within. I create these stories to empower me to stay in joy and peace. I create the stories to stay connected to this experience of spiritual freedom and the immense love within it.

When I create my subjective reality, my subjective story, from a high place of consciousness with the action performed in balance with the worldly situation, I am in this world but not of it.

22

THE SPIRITUAL TRAVELER

Many people believe that their subjective reality about God, their Bible, their version of religion, their sect within their religion is the alpha and omega regarding the subject, and they are the only ones who are saved.

I had to be consciously aware of not getting trapped in this subtle seductive web of vanity, bigotry, arrogance, and self-righteousness. "My religion is better than your religion, or my God is bigger than your God" is, in my opinion, a social consciousness trap. I believe that it captures and closes the heart of many people to the appreciation of the immense beauty that lies within themselves and others.

Observing my opinions on this matter and being indifferent to them helped me to become aware of this mental imprisonment and to avoid it. My perception is that everyone's religious experience is divinely correct for them. People are exactly where they need to be in soul's journey back into the heart of God.

Being raised as a devout Catholic and interacting with devout Christians, I believe there is a close similarity in the interpreting of the message of Jesus, the Christ. From my investigation and experience, his message has been re-created, rewritten, modified, and interpreted by the clergy and by political influences to be an excellent way of life.

The teachings of Jesus in the Christian Bible were written to unify the semi-civilized tribal cultures with socially accepted laws of ethics and morality. They were to indoctrinate, change, or modify the pagan beliefs of these tribes with the new doctrines of Christianity.

Over time, new interpretations were promoted which led to new and unique individual religions and Christian sects. I have noticed that practically all of their beliefs lie within the laws of the universal Christ or universal mind consciousness. Most modern-day religious sects have similar concepts, but they have their own slant and approach that was formed, developed, and propagated to its followers.

From my experiences of knowing the Scriptures and participating in the Catholic rituals, I find they soothe the spirit of their followers with a faith that all is well if they lived within their rules. However, for me, all was well within that small cage of social consciousness.

It was not until Divine Spirit opened the doors through these three aforementioned social injustice experiences that I was propelled out of the cage of social consciousness and rules of mind reality into my own version of mind-created reality and later into the vastness of soul reality.

At first, I used the same set of variables, the same set of rules of the universal mind consciousness which the establishment used to create and propagate their story of reality. I chose to create a different story from the same facts. I found that there are many more possibilities available from the same set of facts than what they were presenting.

I have noted that the carrot that entices people to stay true and not deviate from the limiting propagated version and stories of reality was the faith and security they had in their religious beliefs. There is the future reward of heaven and the fear of what should happen if they disobey. One choice was eternal heavenly entitlement of the good life in heaven verse the eternal pains of hell.

Those three seemingly negative experiences of social injustice mentioned in the first part of the book, which at first appeared negative, were actually huge incentives and opportunities that allowed me to experience spiritual freedom and beauty unlike anything I had ever imagined.

Every soul's journey of emancipation from salvation has the hands of God guiding it. Most everyone has a story about how certain events or experiences were the wake-up call to validate their out-of-the box beliefs and to accelerate their unique journey to heaven.

Every religion is God's gift to soul. Every religion and sect in a religion seems to have their unique blend of both the left-brain mental concepts with the right-brain mystical and spiritual experience. God sees that we are born into the appropriate religious experience necessary for us to grow spiritually.

Early on in my childhood innocence regarding spirituality, I would soul journey to regions of immense beauty and love after the Catholic ritual of Holy Communion and Benediction. There

I would see and visit a magnificent blue and silver star that would radiate rapture, peace, and spiritual ecstasy.

As I grew up in the church, I was educated in the catechism of the Catholic religion and its doctrine. Guilt, blame, and shame were introduced into my life, and the mental concept of sin came to dominate my spiritual viewpoint. The concept of unworthiness and damnation clouded my vision of that magnificent love from this blue star of my youth.

What my mind was being taught and what my heart and soul knew were in conflict. This internal battle persisted for years, until I rejected the mental molds of the church and reinvented my own religious beliefs. These beliefs were within the domain of universal mind consciousness. However, this was the important first step of emancipation for me.

When I was in my early twenties, my next breakthrough came during my year-long sojourn to Hawaii, in one of those long and deep valleys on the island of Oahu. The spiritual consciousness of Hawaii is unique, with the acceptance of many different philosophies and concepts of religions. It is the Hawaiian way.

There, submerged in this wonderful culture and environment, my heart and mind became unified and free of stress. I started to revisit the beautiful places of my childhood prayers after Holy Communion and the Benediction ceremony. Thus, I started my return journey back into the Sacred Heart of God.

Gradually, new and more expansive and free ideals were developing. It was easier to listen to the whisper of Spirit and to become aware of the spiritual realities that were coming into focus. It was in this environment I began to experience and study the art and science of the soul journey. I was not the best of students, but I was persistent because I liked how I felt in my own skin. Likewise, the studies paralleled the spiritual concepts that I was inventing while listening to my heart.

For twentysome years, I was led through the maze of my emotions and thoughts, restructuring my postulates to match my growing spiritual awareness. It was a slow but carefully balanced metamorphosis.

It was not until the clinical incident in Oklahoma and the witnessing of unethical schemes, dirty politics, and lies, with the under-the-table power plays, that I realized it was time to get going. It was time for major changes. That was when it became more important to pay attention to my spiritual growth and less attention to my position in society as the healer extraordinaire. That was what motivated me to put the accelerator to the floor and make my spiritual emancipation a top priority.

Later, I realized the hand of God was at work for those twentysome years, building the foundation for my spiritual launch.

The final touches to the launchpad were the increased urgency of living in the now, attention to the information gathered by my spiritual eye and my spiritual heart, and developing the use of my right brain. The glue that joined all of these disciplines together for my spiritual emancipation from the universal mind consciousness to spiritual freedom became the art and science of soul journey.

This was the modus, the primary spiritual exercises that brought the quickest, the most balanced, and the longest lasting results to aid me on my journey back into the Sacred Heart of God.

During this process, I learned that the vehicle of the soul journey needs a guidance system and fuel. Without both of these ingredients, I realized that I could go nowhere.

When I started to learn soul journeying, I realized that I was operating in a new domain, where there are different laws, rules, and postulates governing this exploration.

When I was a child, I was taught and believed that there are guardian angels looking after us and protecting us. When I started to soul journey, my guardian angel was replaced with spiritual travelers.

Spiritual travelers are souls who are adept at the journey of soul through the physical, mental, emotional, and spiritual planes or dimensions. They have made the journey themselves under the guidance, protection, and love from their spiritual travelers and have mastered the disciplines. They are there to help guide those souls whose time has come to leave the physical, mental, and emotional planes behind. The phrase "be in the world and not of it" became an in-your-face reality.

In my experience, it is nearly impossible to make the journey into the highest heavens without the help of the spiritual travelers. They served as a GPS that guided me in the right direction. The spiritual travelers pointed the way and informed me about the obstacles and dangers. But I had to do the work. It surely is nice to know that they are always there for me.

Developing the awareness of their presence and the ability to use this inner guidance and to create this loving and trusting relationship with spiritual travelers took me on an interesting adventure. The presence of these beautiful spiritual beings is an example of unconditional love, huge spiritual power in presence, and an unwavering loyalty to Divine Spirit. They are steadfast in their mission to help souls gain spiritual freedom and spiritual awareness.

Remember, we are talking about spirituality, not religion. We are dealing with the laws of soul, not the laws of the mind. It is impossible to explain the total academics of this subject because it is too vast. I have mentioned only certain subjects throughout this discourse. It is worth the time and effort to investigate this domain of information for yourself.

Another important job of the spiritual traveler besides being the guide, the GPS function, was to be sure I became aware of the spiritual light and spiritual melodies, sounds, or essence of the different spiritual planes as we passed through.

This part of their job is necessary, for the light and spiritual sound is the nectar of heaven. It is the essence of Divine Spirit. It is the fuel for the vehicle in a soul journey. Without it, there is no travel. It is the reason. It is the Lexus. It is the purifier. It is the magnet that attracts soul. It is the beauty that compels. It is the freedom that abounds within. It is the power. It is the Word, which draws soul to it.

Soul is the driver. Soul journey is the vehicle. The spiritual traveler is the GPS and the ambassador, but the spiritual light and spiritual sound is the fuel. We now are fully equipped ready to travel.

The spiritual traveler has the authority to open doors for soul that no one else can. They have the authority over the gatekeepers of the different spiritual regions. In my opinion, they are absolutely necessary, especially if you want to go beyond the mind.

There is a saying in the metaphysical disciplines that when soul develops to a certain point in its emancipation, the circumstances for soul to find and accept a spiritual traveler will be presented countless times. There is always a spiritual traveler ready to escort soul through the heavens. But there is one requirement: You must accept the gift and surrender. This is the rule of engagement. As I said earlier, the spiritual traveler will guide you and open the door for you, but you have to walk through it.

When I made the commitment to launch, I found something beyond my greatest religious experience with the Christ consciousness. This is not to minimize my earlier religious experiences, for without them I would not have had the courage to follow the light of Christ until it led me to the spiritual traveler. It was the spiritual traveler who gave me the knowing of the sound, the Word, the unspoken yet spiritually audible voice of God. It was that sound that engulfed my soul with its magical, mystical, loving power that led me back to heaven.

I did not have to immediately give up anything that I held dear. There were the additions of many beautiful spiritual qualities that surpassed what I had. I joyfully chose to exchange one postulate for another, one story for another.

This exchange was initiated primarily because I had mystical and spiritual experiences that were beyond the mental concepts of religious doctrines. These experiences were explained and written about by mystics and spiritual travelers. These experiences opened my heart to the awareness of the sublime love of Divine Spirit.

As my soul journey experiences became more real, I operated in a completely different morphic field of reality. Knowing integrated and superseded knowledge. I was living from the consciousness of the open spiritual heart instead of the religious mental concept and associated emotions.

There is a small percentage of people in every religion or sect who have developed a very beautiful and mystical relationship with God. There is also a small percentage of people who have abandoned the mental and emotional concepts of organized religion and followed their heart into a loving relationship with God. Even though the percentage is small, the number of people ready for emancipation from social consciousness into spiritual consciousness is huge.

Hopefully, this book will embellish or validate your spiritual concepts and assist you in taking another step into the Sacred Heart of God. I hope this book will help make your relationship with Divine Spirit an everyday reality and experience. May this book also help you deepen your loving relationship with whoever you choose to call your spiritual master.

For the many Christians who have proclaimed that they are already saved, it is time to walk the walk into the light and then into the sound of God. It is the deep burning fire of that mystical love that will give you the courage to abandon the subtle traps of religious beliefs, to forsake these mental concepts for the real thing.

You can still follow your religion. It is just with repeated soul journey experiences, you will have an increased capacity to love, to be grateful, and to find beauty. Your thoughts, words, and actions would spring from your spiritual heart. They will be organic.

It would not be the beguilements of manipulating people's opinion that will give you the open heart. You do not have to act a certain way or say the right thing in trying to project the outer image of righteousness for social approval. People will know you by the light and spiritual essence or sound that emanates from within your spiritual heart. It is the golden heart that is the golden coin that opens the golden gates to the golden love of Divine Spirit within. It is from that tone of spiritual love that your heart's desire will be to serve life, without any desire for social approval or gratification.

Take the step from experiencing God from the sensation of the mind and body and follow the light into the stillness of the spiritual heart. It is time to have the mystical experience and to stop reading, talking, and theorizing about it. It is time to follow the mystical Jesus and not the legendary biblical Jesus. It is time for the emancipation.

Be totally still. Then for just thirty seconds, totally surrender every mental attachment to any and all religious doctrine. Stop thinking and go beyond the mental and emotional beliefs into the Sacred Heart of God. Take the soul journey with the spiritual traveler. They know how to integrate the mystical love of the light into your essence and then have you experience the glorious sounds of God and the spiritual vortex of Divine Spirit. They are the adepts and the master of helping you blend the imagination with the spiritual eye, the right brain and the now.

For the many that resonate with the knowingness that there is more to what the religious doctrines are saying, this is the moment to consider the spiritual journey. It is time to awaken the knowing that resides within the sacred chambers of your spiritual heart. Ask and it shall be given. Knock and the door will be opened. The spiritual traveler is waiting for you to accept his request.

Printed in the United States
By Bookmasters